The Powers to Lead

The Powers to Lead

Joseph S. Nye Jr.

OXFORD
UNIVERSITY PRESS

2008

OXFORD

UNIVERSITY PRESS

Oxford University Press, Inc., publishes works that further
Oxford University's objective of excellence
in research, scholarship, and education.

Oxford   New York
Auckland   Cape Town   Dar es Salaam   Hong Kong   Karachi
Kuala Lumpur   Madrid   Melbourne   Mexico City   Nairobi
New Delhi   Shanghai   Taipei   Toronto

With offices in
Argentina   Austria   Brazil   Chile   Czech Republic   France   Greece
Guatemala   Hungary   Italy   Japan   Poland   Portugal   Singapore
South Korea   Switzerland   Thailand   Turkey   Ukraine   Vietnam

Published by Oxford University Press, Inc.
198 Madison Avenue, New York, New York 10016

www.oup.com

Oxford is a registered trademark of Oxford University Press

Library of Congress Cataloging-in-Publication Data
Nye, Joseph S.
The powers to lead / Joseph S. Nye.
    p.   cm.
ISBN 978-0-19-533562-0
1. Political leadership.   2. Leadership.   3. Executive ability.
4. Interpersonal communication.   I. Title.
JC330.3.N94 2008
352.23'6—dc22   2007039163

9 8 7 6 5 4 3 2 1

Printed in the United States of America
on acid-free paper

For the Kennedy School students
and colleagues
who have taught me.

And, as always, for Molly,
who leads with soft power.

Contents

Preface

A leader is best when people barely know he exists, not so good when people obey and acclaim him; worst when they despise him.

Lao Tzu, 630 B.C.[1]

One ought to be both feared and loved, but as it is difficult for the two to go together, it is much safer to be feared than loved. . . . Still a prince should make himself feared in such a way that if he does not gain love, he at any rate avoids hatred.

Machiavelli, 1513[2]

Two-thirds of Americans say their country is in a "leadership crisis." They distrust their leaders—whether politician, boardroom chief, university head, or media watchdog. In each of eleven different fields, no more than 40 percent said they had a great deal of confidence in their leaders.[3] Americans have long been ambivalent about leaders, and the problem is not limited to the United States. Polls show similar results in many countries.[4] Those facts might tempt some to shrug off the problem as nothing new, but in reality, the context of leadership is changing, and many of today's leaders have not caught up with it.

Both power and leadership are changing in today's world. Knowledge is power, and more people have more information than at any prior time in human history. A former CEO of a multinational medical instruments company argues that "the time is ripe to redefine leadership for the 21st century. The military-manufacturing model of leadership that worked so well 50 years ago doesn't get the best out of people today."[5] A few decades ago, some theorists contrasted a power approach with a leadership approach.[6] But if one thinks of power as including both the hard power of coercion and the soft power of attraction, leadership and power are inextricably intertwined. President George W. Bush has said, "I'm the decider, and I decide what's best," but there is much more to leadership than that.[7]

Leadership involves power, but not all power relationships are instances of leadership. Bombing an enemy into submission is quite different from attracting others to follow. However, some contemporary theories that define leadership as synonymous with the soft power of attraction miss another part of reality. In practice, effective leadership requires a mixture of soft and hard power skills that I call *smart power*. The proportions differ with contexts. A business executive has more access to the hard power of hiring and firing; a university president or a democratic politician has to rely more on the soft power of attraction and persuasion. I introduced the concept of soft power into the discourse of international politics two decades ago. Now I find others using these terms in discussions of leadership, but not always in the most appropriate way.

This book explores the relationship of hard and soft power to leadership. There are many ways to define leadership. One recent count collected 221 definitions from the 1920s to the 1990s, with the earlier ones stressing the ability of a leader to impress his or her will and later ones seeing more mutuality in the relationship between leaders and followers.[8] I define leaders as those who help a group create and achieve shared goals. Some try to impose their own goals, others derive them more from the group, but leaders mobilize people to reach those objectives. Leadership is a social relationship with three key components—leaders, followers, and the contexts in which they interact—and I will examine each.

A significant strand of current leadership theory is described as the "neocharismatic and transformational approach." Charisma or personal magnetism is an important dimension of the soft power of attraction, but charisma is hard to pin down. The press has described many a political leader or CEO as "charismatic" when things are going well, only to withdraw the label after he or she fails. Transformation is also a difficult term to pin down. President Bush thinks of himself as a transformational leader, and Condoleezza Rice, his secretary of state, has spoken of the administration's "transformational diplomacy." These terms, developed by leadership theorists and used by some leaders, can be confusing because they refer both to leaders' objectives and to the styles they use. In fact, much of current leadership theory is in need of more careful specification.

I found this out the hard way. After five years working at the assistant secretary level in the State Department, the Pentagon, and the Intelligence community and another eight years as a university dean, I thought I had some experience with leadership. After I stepped down as dean in 2004, I agreed to teach a core curriculum course on leadership at the Kennedy School of Government. As I began seriously to read the leadership literature, I could not find a good short analytical introduction about power and leadership for the students I was teaching or for the general reader. There were short introductory books, but they were not analytical. I wanted something based on the scientific and historical record but written in an accessible style.

There is a considerable literature on leadership written by psychologists and experts on organizational behavior, but much of it is not written for a general audience. There is also a large leadership coaching industry that has produced a vast number of books, tapes, and programs that take a how-to and self-help approach, but much of it is analytically weak. In 1990, after surveying hundreds of definitions of leadership, one expert concluded that leadership is a very "hot" word, but it "has come to mean all things to all people."[9] One study counted over six thousand such books on the subject, though the authors commented that they felt they were "reviewing the same book 50 times with different titles."[10] Little of this literature adequately addresses the questions of power and leadership in a context broader than that of modern organizations. I hope to clarify this discussion by applying the concepts of hard and soft power to leadership as I see it. This is the gap I propose to fill with this book: What can I tell people about power and leadership in a short analytical primer so that they can select, evaluate, and judge their leaders? Nothing is more important than citizens having the tools to assess and judge their leaders, whether past or present, public or private. Leadership is an art, not a science, but even art benefits from criticism.

Chapter 1 discusses the ubiquity of leadership in human groups and organizations over time and addresses the causal importance of leaders in history. I distinguish leadership with and without authority, shared leadership, and the role of nature and nurture in forming leaders. Chapter 2 develops my distinction between hard and soft power and applies it to leaders and to followers. I also discuss how power resources change over time and context. Chapter 3 focuses on the types and skills of leaders. I criticize and reformulate the concepts of charismatic and noncharismatic leaders and transformational and transactional leaders and examine the key skills for leadership in modern democratic societies, including the inspirational skills of vision, communication, and emotional IQ, as well as political and organizational skills related to transactions. Chapter 4 outlines the contextual intelligence essential for smart power. I discuss culture, the distribution of power, followers' needs and demands, crisis situations, and information flows. Good contextual intelligence broadens the bandwidth of leaders so that they can develop and adapt strategies for different situations. Finally, chapter 5 addresses good and bad leadership from the point of view of both effectiveness and ethics and why leaders are often held to a different standard. Understanding how better to judge good and bad leaders will be crucial for our democratic future.

Many people have helped me with this short book. I have benefited from observation, discussion, and interviews with a number of American and foreign leaders, some of whom are cited in the notes. I have learned a great deal from my colleagues and students at the Kennedy School. I am particularly grateful for the support of the school's Center for Public Leadership. For helpful comments, I wish to thank Graham Allison, James Blight, Hannah Bowles, Jack Donahue, David Gergen, Richard Hackman, Ron Heifetz, Ben Heineman, Elaine Kamarck, Barbara Kellerman, Nan Keohane, Robert Keohane, Rakesh Khurana, Matthew Kohut, Rod Kramer, Dutch Leonard, Ted Marmor, Mark Moore, Ben Nye, Dan Nye, Molly Nye, Todd Pittinsky, Robert Rotberg, David Welch, Kenneth Winston, Andrew Zelleke, and Peter Zimmerman. I had wonderful research assistance from Henry Walters and Mark Fliegauf, and overall support from Jeanne Marasca. I stand on the shoulders of others and am blessed by their friendship.

ONE

Leadership

Leadership is changing—or so we are told. The information revolution is transforming politics and organizations. Hierarchies are becoming flatter and embedded in fluid networks of contacts. Most workers in postindustrial societies are knowledge workers, and they respond to different incentives and political appeals than did the industrial workers of the past century. Polls show that people today are less deferential to authority in organizations and in politics. Soft power is becoming more important.

The CEO of Google says he has to "coddle" his employees, and another Silicon Valley executive explains that with an educated workforce and free flow of information, "if I don't treat my employees with respect and involve them in decision-making, they will walk down the street to some start-up that has an interesting story."[1] Even the military faces these changes. The Pentagon says that American army drillmasters do "less shouting at everyone" because today's generation responds better to instructors who play "a more counseling type role."[2] Military success against terrorists and counterinsurgents requires soldiers to win hearts and minds, not just break bodies. Management experts report that their studies observe "an increase in the use of more participative processes."[3] Leadership theorists speak of "shared leadership" and "distributed leadership." They suggest images of leaders in the center of a circle rather than atop a hierarchy.

At least that is the new conventional wisdom about those who occupy authoritative political and organizational positions in postmodern societies. Some say leadership will be increasingly a "woman's world." Leadership research on gender reports the increased success of what was once considered a "feminine style of leadership." In terms of gender stereotypes, the masculine leadership style is assertive, competitive, authoritarian, and focused on commanding the behavior of others. The feminine style is collaborative, participatory, integrative, and aimed at co-opting the behavior of followers.

Not everyone agrees. The Stanford psychologist Roderick Kramer warns that "in all our recent enchantment with social intelligence and soft power, we've overlooked the kinds of skills leaders need to bring about transformation in cases of tremendous resistance or inertia." Although some studies suggest that bullying is detrimental to organizational performance, Kramer describes bullies who have a vision and disdain social constraints as "great intimidators." And they often succeed.[4] So where do we stand on leadership today?

Mistrust of leaders is not a new problem. Three decades ago, experts were asking "Where have all the leaders gone?"[5] In part, such attitudes reflect the golden glow of the past. The present is never like the good old days. Studies by psychologists show that people regularly rate dead leaders more highly than living leaders.[6] But another part of the answer is that people are looking in the wrong places. Leadership is ubiquitous, and leaders are all around us. People persist in looking for heroic leaders—a Mount Rushmore syndrome—although leadership is actually much more broadly distributed in societies. If we focus too much on leaders, the resulting cult of individual personality devalues communities and undercuts the distributed leadership that makes them run. A Canadian expert urges, "Let us get rid of this cult of leadership."[7]

DO LEADERS MATTER?

Skeptics deny that leaders matter all that much. People easily make the mistake of "leader attribution error."[8] We see something going right or wrong with a group or organization and then attribute the result to the leader. He or she becomes a scapegoat, even while being more a symbol of failure than its cause. Sports teams fire coaches after a losing season whether or not they are blameworthy. Business executives lose their jobs after profits turn down; others get credit for success in bull markets. Voters reward and punish politicians for economic conditions that often were created before the leaders took office.

In the presence of multiple causes and random events, attributing blame or praise to a person can provide a sense of psychological comfort and reassurance about our ability to understand and control events in a complex and confusing world. Primitive peoples' belief in magic provided them with a reassuring sense of control over such crucial events as disease and storms, which they were actually impotent to affect. The modern political arena offers a similar illusion: "Belief in a political leader's ability to alter affairs may generate a feeling of indirect control. The ability to reward or punish incumbents through the vote implies this influence."[9] Various experiments have shown that the desire to make sense of confusing events leads to a romanticized, larger-than-life role for leaders, particularly in extreme cases of very good or very bad performance.[10]

How much do leaders really matter? Studies of organizations show mixed results. For example, General Electric prides itself on training leaders. Rising managers must attend a leadership training course at a special school in Crotonville, New York, and though only a few will make it to the top of GE, the company boasts that its alumni often become leaders of other companies. How well do these GE alumni do as CEOs of other companies? About half succeed and half fail.[11] That is better than we would expect from a group selected at random, but far from perfect.

A Harvard Business School study of the effects of CEOs on corporate performance in forty-two industries shows that on average the effect of the CEO accounted for about 14 percent of the difference in performance, ranging from 2 percent in the meat processing industry to 21 percent in telecommunications.[12] A study of forty-six college and university presidents found that the role of the leader was largely a myth, and a study of the effects of mayors on city budgets came to a similar conclusion.[13] Another study of service teams at Xerox found that the way teams were designed accounted for 42 percent of the variance in success; less than 10 percent was attributable to the qualities of their leaders' coaching abilities.[14] On the one hand, any variable (such as leadership) that accounts for 10 percent of the variation of complex social phenomena is a factor to be reckoned with. On the other hand, these findings hardly support the magical view of causation popularly attributed to leaders!

Of course, such studies have their limits. They tell us about averages over numerous cases, but sometimes a leader can make a large difference and beat the averages in a particular case. Moreover, these studies focus on institutions with well-established procedures for recruitment and promotion, and leaders who already hold positions of authority. Leaders are already well sorted before they reach the top, and the oddballs, deviants, and geniuses have been excluded well before that. Social movement leaders like Gandhi and Martin Luther King Jr. would not have made it to the top of GE, nor is it likely they would have done well if by some chance they had. Formal organizations are an important slice of life, but only a slice. Many leadership contexts are far more fluid, whether they are political groups, street gangs, universities, or online communities. Leading inside an institution is different from leading a movement without institutions. A prophetic style fits well with a loosely organized social movement, whereas managerial competence is important in an organization. In social movements, we might expect leaders to count for more (and in the case of online communities, less) than in corporate life. Conclusions drawn from studies of organizational behavior (which is the focus of the majority of academic and business studies) may not tell us much about these other dimensions of leadership.

HISTORY LESSONS

This raises the age-old question of the role of leaders in history. For centuries, history was written as the record of the doings of great men. Thomas Carlyle wrote in 1840, "The history of what man has accomplished in this world, is at bottom the History of the Great Men who have worked here" (although a skeptical Herbert Spencer pointed out in 1873, "Before he can re-make his society, his society must make him").[15] Perhaps the best summary of this insoluble problem came from Karl Marx: "Men make their own history, but they do not make it as they please . . . but under circumstances existing already, given and transmitted from the past."[16]

It seems obvious that Alexander the Great, Julius Caesar, Genghis Khan, Louis XIV, and Winston Churchill all made a difference in history, but it is much harder to say how much. History is an imperfect laboratory, and controlled experiments that hold other variables constant are impossible. Time and context have a huge impact. For example, President George W. Bush frequently refers to Churchill, whom many historians describe as one of the greatest leaders of the twentieth century. But at the beginning of 1940, Churchill was widely regarded as a washed-up backbench member of Parliament. As a conservative British prime minister said in 1936, "While we delight to listen to him in this House, we do not take his advice."[17] Churchill would have been a minor figure in the history books if Hitler had not invaded France in May 1940. Then Churchill became the man who fit the moment. Churchill did not change; the context changed. Without Hitler's actions, Churchill would not be seen today as a great leader. Or to take a more recent example, Rudolph Giuliani (who also takes Churchill as his role model) has enjoyed a reputation for leadership (and written a book with that title) based on his actions following September 11, 2001. Before that tragedy, he was known as a mayor with a mixed record. He did well on crime but poorly on race relations. On September 10, he seemed to have little political future. But his ability to interpret events and calm a fearful public after the attack, particularly in the absence of the president, projected him as a great leader and helped to relaunch a political career that includes a run for the presidency.

The philosopher Sidney Hook once tried to sort out this question by distinguishing "eventful vs. event-making" leaders. An eventful leader influences the course of subsequent developments by his actions. In Hook's metaphor, the mythical little Dutch boy who stuck his finger in a leaking dike and saved his country was an eventful leader, but any little boy or any finger could have done the trick. An event-making leader, on the other hand, doesn't just find a fork in the historical road: he helps to create it.[18] Such leaders are called *transformational* in the sense of changing what would otherwise be the course of history. They raise new issues and new questions. "Good politicians win the argument. Every now and then someone comes along and changes it."[19] Margaret Thatcher and Tony Blair were not universally liked as prime ministers in Britain, but both were credited with changing the political weather.

Up until 1938, Adolf Hitler's role in the origins and outcome of World War II was more eventful than transformational. Many of the German ultranationalists cast up by the conditions of the 1930s held similar views and might have taken similar actions. But after 1938, Hitler became transformational. His immoral and risky choices created new conditions that led to the deaths of millions and devastation for his nation. After September 11, 2001, any American president might have responded to the Taliban government's provision of sanctuary to Al Qaeda in Afghanistan, but in choosing to also invade Iraq, George W. Bush created a fork in the road and became a transformational rather than merely eventful leader.[20]

Consider the end of the cold war and the breakup of the Soviet Union, one of the great events of the late twentieth century that some Americans attribute to the tough rhetoric and military budgets of President Ronald Reagan. In the American mythology, "With a mighty shove (or a kick in the pants), he was destined to send the Soviets reeling toward the 'ash-heap' of history."[21] Yet although Reagan's actions had some effect and he was eventful, he did not create the fork in the historical road. Causation was far more complex. The most important underlying cause was the failure of the centrally planned Soviet economy to adapt to the information economy (the "third industrial revolution"). If Yuri Andropov, a tough KGB-based Soviet leader, had not died, Reagan's rhetoric might have been to little avail. Reagan was fortunate that Mikhail Gorbachev came to power in 1985. By

launching his program of *perestroika* and *glasnost,* designed to reform and preserve the Soviet Union, Gorbachev actually accelerated the inevitable decline by a decade or so. Moreover, by
choosing not to use force to resist the decline of the Soviet empire,
he (and Boris Yeltsin) hastened the collapse of the Soviet Union.
In explaining why the cold war ended when it did, Reagan was
eventful, but Gorbachev was transformational. Ironically, however, Gorbachev did not create the transformation he intended
(which was to save the Soviet Union).[22] When the bureaucrats
resisted his perestroika, or structural reforms, he tried to light a fire
under them by increasing glasnost, or open criticism. But when
people were allowed to say what they wanted, many wanted to be
out of the Soviet Union. Like a person who starts pulling a loose
thread to improve the appearance of his sweater, he wound up
unraveling the whole thing.

Assassination might be thought of as one brutal historical test of
the importance of a leader, particularly in the case of amorphous
social movements whose prophetic leaders often lack clear suc-
cessors. Sometimes removing a leader destroys a social movement;
at other times, it does not. Mahatma Gandhi and Martin Luther
King Jr. became influential martyrs. On the other hand, the
military government of Nigeria was able to thoroughly disrupt the
Movement for the Survival of the Ogoni People when they executed its charismatic leader, Ken Saro-Wiwa (and eight others),
in 1995 despite Saro-Wiwa's broad international connections. In
contrast, when the government of El Salvador arranged the killing
of Archbishop Romero in 1980, it had the effect of stimulating the
movement for social change in the country. Careful studies show
that the difference lies in conditions in the country and in the
movement as much as the individuals involved.[23]

Leaders have different degrees of effect on history, which are not
captured by Hook's oversimplified distinction, and transformational

change is often a matter of degree. Leaders matter "a little more, a little less, depending on how they diagnose those problem situations for their political communities, what responses they prescribe for meeting them, and how well they mobilize the political community's support for their decisions."[24] We know that leaders matter more in some conditions than in others, particularly in fluid times of crisis, but getting the details of causation right provides work for generations of historians. Because each age has access to new facts, incorporates new biases, and raises new questions, even careful judgments change over time. Theodore Roosevelt was a popular president who brought American foreign policy into the twentieth century. In contrast, Woodrow Wilson's foreign policy of promoting democracy and the League of Nations was a failure and was rejected by the American people for two decades after his death. Nonetheless, Henry Kissinger argues that by the middle of the century, Wilson's ideas had more influence on American opinion than did Teddy Roosevelt's.[25] As we shall see, however, generating influential ideas is not the same as mobilizing people for action.

A careful study of change in U.S. government concludes that policies sometimes change in "very large leaps, as in the New Deal of the 1930s, the Great Society of the mid-1960s, and the Reagan revolution of 1981." Obviously, Franklin Roosevelt, Lyndon Johnson, and Ronald Reagan played important roles in these events as the policy entrepreneurs who took advantage of events and coupled politics with ideas to produce significant change. In that sense, they were transformational leaders. But to see these transformations as the product of great men alone "neglects patterns in events." Leaders and policy entrepreneurs are like surfers waiting for a big wave: "Individuals do not control waves, but can ride them. Individuals do not control events or structures, but can anticipate them and bend them to their purpose to some degree."[26] Events create windows of opportunity, which may close in a relatively short period. Many opportunities for change go unfulfilled. Leaders matter when they have the intuition and skills to take advantage of those windows while they are open.

HEROIC AND ALPHA MALE APPROACHES TO LEADERSHIP

The fact that history has been written in terms of heroes constrains our imagination and understanding of the enormous potential of human leadership that ranges from Attila the Hun to Mother Teresa. Most everyday leaders remain unheralded. And the heroic approach neglects the community norms and institutions that provide crucial constraints on leaders. James Madison and the framers of the U.S. Constitution understood the importance of institutions in shaping and constraining how "men make history." They knew that Plato's search for a philosopher king or Carlyle's advice—"Find in any country the Ablest Man that exists there; raise him to the supreme place, and loyally reverence him; you have a perfect government for that country"[27]—is fraught with risk. Humans seek heroes, but not all heroes are leaders, and not all leaders are heroic.[28]

Neither the ancient Greeks nor the Romans who influenced Western civilization had an abstract noun that denoted "leadership" as we use it today. To lead (*agein* in Greek; *ducere* in Latin) was originally a military term meaning "to be general of soldiers." Western civilization's paradigmatic ideal of a leader grew out of Homer's *Iliad* and *Odyssey*, an ideal of the brave warrior leading by example in the Trojan War. The role of heroic leadership in war led to overemphasis of command and control and hard military power. The ancient image of the leader as warrior persists to this day. A study of twentieth-century rulers found that more than half "had a chance to show their military prowess either as aggressors or defenders."[29] Even in modern America, presidential greatness (and failure) has been correlated with wartime presidencies.

The role of the warrior leader is not finished. The writer Robert Kaplan points to the birth of a new "warrior class as cruel as ever and better armed," ranging from Russian Mafiosi to Latin American drug kingpins and terrorists who glorify the thrill of violence, just as the ancient Greeks did in the sacking of Troy.[30] Kaplan argues that modern leaders must respond in kind. Modern leadership demands a pagan ethos rooted in the past.

Smart warriors, however, know how to lead with more than just the use of force. Part of ancient Chinese wisdom is represented by Sun-Tzu, who wrote *The Art of Warfare* six centuries before the Christian era and concluded that the highest excellence is never having to fight because the commencement of battle signifies a political failure. Soldiers sometimes joke that their job description is simple: kill people and break things. In practice, military leadership is more complex. According to American generals in Iraq, military force alone cannot produce victory: "It's very important— you have to interact with the people."[31] Hearts and minds matter, and smart warriors understand the soft power of attraction as well as the hard power of coercion. Indeed, an oversimplified image of warrior-style leadership has caused costly setbacks for America's role in the world in the first decade of the twenty-first century. It is not a manly modern Achilles or the strongest alpha male who makes the best warrior leader in today's communication age. Military leadership today requires political and managerial skills. As one recent study concludes, "An increasingly important component of military leadership is management of civilians and contractors."[32] Generals today use words more than swords.

Of course, at various times and places, fear has worked. As Xenophon explained the success of Cyrus the Great in ruling his empire twenty-five hundred years ago, "He was able to cover so vast a region with the fear which he inspired, that he struck all men with terror and no one tried to withstand him; and he was able to awaken in all so lively a desire to please him, that they always wished to be guided by his will."[33] Stalin was a master of control by terror.[34] Many autocratic rulers—in Zimbabwe, Burma, and Belarus, among others—still lead in such a fashion today. Others combine fear with corruption to maintain kleptocracies dominated by the big man and his coterie.[35] A good portion of the two hundred countries in the world is ruled that way.

Some theorists have tried to explain this with an alpha male theory of leadership. The psychiatrist Arnold M. Ludwig, for example, argues that just as male monkeys, chimps, and apes automatically begin to assume more responsibility for their particular community once they attain the dominant status of alpha male, human rulers begin to do so as well. "The reason that would-be leaders are always ready to try their hand at ruling seems to be because they have little other choice. . . . Any vacuum in leadership seems to unleash powerful social and biological forces within potential candidates to ensure that any power void will not exist for too long. . . . The tendency for this response seems coded in their genes and represents a latent archetypal response in much the same way as male chimps and baboons must challenge the existing leader whenever they sense they have the slightest chance to win—and often even when they do not."[36]

Humans share over 98 percent of our genome with chimpanzees, tool-using animals that live in groups dominated by alpha males. It is also true that "social living depends on authority [and] authority relationships resemble the dominance and deference relationships of our primate ancestors."[37] Humans work out pecking orders just like other animals. In the eighteenth century Samuel Johnson pointed out, "No two people can be half an hour together, but one shall acquire an evident superiority over the other." The primate specialists Richard Wrangham and Dale Peterson conclude that pride, which is a great source of conflict, "evolved during countless generations in which males who achieved high status were able to turn their social success into extra reproduction."[38] People are constantly playing games, literally and metaphorically, to establish dominance in status.

However, such sociobiological explanations of leadership are of only limited value. Thus far, no leadership gene has been identified, and studies of identical and fraternal male twins suggest that only a third of their difference in occupying formal leadership roles can be accounted for by genetic factors.[39] While this suggests that inbred characteristics influence the extent to which people play particular roles, it leaves lots of room for people to learn behavior that influences outcomes. The alpha male theory of leadership also fails some other tests. Although humans are one of the 150 species of primates, all of which reproduce slowly and live in groups, "scientists cannot reasonably assume that primate society has a basic nature because there is no longer one basic primate society."[40]

In groups of bonobos (once considered pygmy chimpanzees but in fact a separate species that lives in the Congo), males are not very aggressive and females often play a dominant role in the social system. Bonobos are also less aggressive and warlike than chimpanzees in their reactions to neighboring groups. And although humans are slightly closer genetically to chimpanzees, that may not always lead to xenophobia. The amygdala region of human brains that regulates fear and aggression is hardwired to react to strangers, but people can be trained to accept diversity so that their amygdala does not activate fight-or-flight responses when exposed to strangers.[41]

Humans diverged from the other four families of great apes long ago. Our last common ancestor lived over 5 million years ago. Throughout 99 percent of human history, we lived in small groups of hunters and gatherers. Settled agriculture began only in the Neolithic age, a mere 10,000 years ago. And along with agriculture came hierarchy in human groups. As anthropologists have discovered, most hunter-gatherer groups that exist today tend to be relatively egalitarian, at least among males, and do not have patterns of alpha male dominance. They have "situational leadership" in which the leader varies with the group's circumstances. Seniority exists, but there is nothing that even approaches the idea of a chief or Big Man. As described by the anthropologist Christopher Boehm, "The rank and file, watching leaders with special care, keep them from developing any serious degree of authority."[42]

That leads to a paradox. Perhaps the hunter-gatherer societies that remain today are atypical cultures that were inclined to retreat to niches when pressed by the rise of agriculture and industry. But if these remnants are typical of earlier hunter-gatherers, then the history of human hierarchy is a U-shaped curve with a high degree of inequality existing when we had a common ancestor with the apes and again after we settled down to farm, but not for most of our history in between.[43] If humans are hardwired by nature to be led by alpha males, how do we explain the possibility that for most of our genetic history we had no alpha males? Or that some human cultures today still have no such leaders?

NATURE AND NURTURE

Another effect of the traditional heroic approach to leadership has been to support the belief that leaders are born rather than made, and that nature is more important than nurture. This belief focuses our attention on the selection rather than training of leaders. Indeed, the search for the essential traits of a leader dominated the field of leadership studies until the late 1940s and remains popular in common discourse today. How often have you heard someone say that a political candidate looks (or does not look) like a leader? A tall handsome person enters a room, draws attention, and "looks like a leader." Various studies have shown that tall men are often favored, and corporate CEOs are taller than average. Moreover, tall men tend to earn more than shorter men. Other things being equal, among males "an inch of height is worth $789 a year in salary."[44] But some of the most powerful leaders in history, such as Napoleon, Stalin, and Teng Hsiao-p'ing, were little over five feet tall. Physical traits such as physique, intellectual traits such as IQ, and personality traits such as extroversion have been extensively examined by researchers, but with poor explanatory results. "While studies might find a certain trait to be significant, there always seemed to be considerable evidence that failed to confirm that trait's importance."[45] Context is often more important than traits. The athletic child who is the natural leader on the playground may lose that dominant position when the group returns to a well-structured classroom. As we saw earlier, Churchill's traits did not change in 1940; the situation did.

The traits-centered approach has not vanished from studies of leadership, but it has been broadened and made more flexible. Traits have come to be seen as consistent patterns of personality rather than inherited characteristics.[46] This definition mixes nature and nurture and means that traits can to some extent be learned rather than merely inherited. We talk about leaders being more energetic, more willing to take risks, more optimistic, more persuasive, and more empathetic than other people, but these traits are affected partly by a leader's genetic makeup and partly by the environments in which the traits were learned and developed. A nice experiment recently demonstrated the interaction between nature and nurture. A group of employers was asked to hire workers who had been ranked by their looks. If the employers saw only the individuals' résumés, beauty had no impact on hiring.

Surprisingly, however, when telephone interviews were included in the process, beautiful people did better even though unseen by the employers. A lifetime of social reinforcement based on their genetic looks may have encoded into their voice patterns a tone of confidence that could be projected over the phone. Nature and nurture became thoroughly intertwined.[47]

Genetics and biology matter in human leadership, but they do not determine it in the way that the traditional heroic approach to leadership suggests. The Big Man type of leadership works well in societies based on networks of tribal cultures that rely on personal and family honor and loyalty. Some argue that these leadership patterns remain characteristic of many Arab societies today.[48] Other analysts argue that such social structures are archaic and are not well adapted for coping with today's complex information-based world. In their view, institutional constraints such as constitutions and impartial legal systems must circumscribe such heroic figures. Otherwise, such societies that rest on heroic leaders will not be able to develop the civil society and broad social capital that are necessary for leading in today's networked world.[49] If this is true, modern postheroic leadership turns out to be less about who you are or into which family you were born than about what you have learned and what you do as part of a group. Nature and nurture intertwine, but nurture is much more important in the modern world than the heroic paradigm gives it credit for.

DEFINING LEADERS AND LEADERSHIP

In the late 1990s, members of the editorial board of *Time* magazine debated whom they would put on the January 2000 cover as the most important person of the twentieth century. They narrowed their list to Churchill, Franklin D. Roosevelt, Mahatma Gandhi, and Albert Einstein. They picked Einstein as the person whose extraordinary creativity had the greatest impact on the age, but, unlike the others, Einstein was not a leader. In the words of former *Time* editor and Einstein biographer Walter Isaacson, Einstein was a landmark but not a beacon. He cared little about followers and trained few graduate students. He was not a recluse, he enjoyed his celebrity, but he declined the presidency of Israel as well as of Brandeis University because he sensed that he did not have the interests or skills to be a leader. He had spent a lifetime flaunting authority and going his own way and regarded it as ironic that he should become an authority.[50] As he wrote to a friend in 1949, "I am generally regarded as a sort of petrified object. I find this role not too distasteful, as it corresponds very well with my temperament. . . . I . . . do not take myself nor the doings of the masses seriously, am not ashamed of my weaknesses and vices, and naturally take things as they come with equanimity and humor."[51]

Of course, Einstein was a leader in the simple sense of making breakthrough scientific discoveries that others followed, but like the front-runner in a race, he was not much interested in those who followed. He was a thought leader, just as Beethoven was a musical leader. Once they had written or composed, no one could do physics or compose music as it had been done before. That is a different sense of leadership than being the leader of a human group. Compare Einstein to Abraham Lincoln. Einstein's efforts to promote arms control and world government after World War II were well intentioned, but largely ineffectual in attracting followers. Garry Wills points out that Lincoln "had to understand the mix of motives in his fellow citizens, the counterbalancing intensities with which the different positions were held, and in what directions they were changing, moment by moment."[52] Lincoln was a master of understanding both large political trends in the national body politic as well as how to get the best performance out of the small "team of rivals" he had appointed to his cabinet.[53]

A leader needs to understand followers: "This is the time-consuming aspect of leadership. It explains why great thinkers and artists are rarely the leaders of others (as opposed to influences on them)." Moreover, the scientist does not adjust his or her views to the audience in the way that "Lincoln trimmed and hedged on slavery in order to make people take small steps in the direction of facing the problem."[54]

As noted in the preface, I am interested in leadership that involves relationships of power within groups. A quick look at any dictionary shows that many definitions of leaders and leadership exist, but our most common usage focuses on a person who guides or is in charge of others, and that implies followers who move in the same direction. Leadership means mobilizing people for a purpose. Suppose a little girl in a group sitting by a swimming pool gets up and dives in. She is not a leader if none of the other kids follow suit. Leadership of human groups is not defined by a loner going first and taking risks, no matter how bold or creative. It is a relationship that orients and mobilizes followers. Rosa Parks was not the first African American woman to refuse to give up her seat on a segregated bus in Montgomery, Alabama, in 1955. In October, Mary Louise Smith was jailed for a similar offense, but the local chapter of the NAACP decided that her family background made her a poor test case against segregation. Nor did Rosa Parks go to work on December 1, 1955, primed for a showdown. However, as someone who had worked with the local NAACP, she fully understood the broader implications of her action for others. Her emphatic refusal to budge in the face of a concrete injustice combined with her status in the local community meant that her act of principled civil disobedience unleashed a legion of followers.[55]

I define a leader as someone who helps a group create and achieve shared goals. The shared objectives are important. The children of Hamelin followed the legendary Pied Piper to oblivion when he wreaked his revenge upon the town in the thirteenth century, but he was not a leader in the sense of helping a group set and achieve shared goals. Millions of people closely watch the televised antics of the heiress Paris Hilton, and some even buy products that bear her name. That makes her a celebrity, but self-promotion is not leadership. Other celebrities such as the rock star Bono use their renown to set and advance group goals, such as aid to Africa. That makes them leaders as well as celebrities. Some celebrities fall on the borderline of leadership. For example, music icons like Madonna articulate and conceptualize feminism. This leads to "a form of emotional mobilization that empowers young feminists, but it does not lead to wide-scale mobilization."[56]

The leader need not be a single individual, and the goals may be derived from the group, but leadership is the power to orient and mobilize others for a purpose. Some leaders act with the formal authority of a position such as president or chair; others act without formal authority, as Rosa Parks did.[57] In the struggle for India's independence, Jawaharlal Nehru led with his authority as head of the Congress Party, yet Mahatma Gandhi generally led without formal authority. Sometimes those holding the formal positions are not the true leaders in a group. The British monarch has less power than the prime minister; many a committee chair presides over but does not initiate change in a group. I found when I first entered government as a political appointee that many civil servants were happy to do what they wanted while politely presenting me with faits accomplis if I let them. Holding a formal leadership position is like having a fishing license; it does not guarantee you will catch any fish.

Leadership is not just who you are but what you do. The functions that leaders perform for human groups are to create meaning and goals, reinforce group identity and cohesion, provide order, and mobilize collective work.[58] In a careful study of work teams, Richard Hackman found that the functions of leaders are setting a compelling direction, fine-tuning a team's structure, and providing resource support and expert coaching: "Team leadership can be—and, at its best, often is—a *shared* activity. Anyone and everyone who clarifies a team's direction, or improves its structure, or secures organizational supports for it, or provides coaching that improves its performance processes is providing team leadership."[59]

The test of a leader is whether a group is more effective in both defining and achieving its goals because of that person's participation. The modern military tries to inculcate leadership in all ranks. An orchestra has not only a conductor, but also a concertmaster. Some chamber orchestras work without conductors, and some jazz groups shift the lead constantly.[60] In corporations, truly coequal leadership such as at Hewlett-Packard in its early days may be relatively rare, but there are numerous instances of shared leadership in a right-hand man division of labor such as that between Bill Gates and Steve Ballmer at Microsoft.[61] Patterns of sharing often change over the life cycle of a firm: "Individuals will assume a leadership role as attention turns from one task to another."[62] Not only are leaders and followers often interchangeable in small groups, but in large groups and organizations, most people wind up leading from the middle, serving as leaders and followers—principals and agents—at the same time. Such followers help their bosses to lead as well as provide leadership for their own followers. Leadership can be broadly distributed within groups and can shift with situations.[63] Some radical groups (such as the environmental group Earth First!) pride themselves on being "leaderless," but that is because they make the mistake of equating leadership with formal authority.[64]

We can think of leadership as a process with three key components: leaders, followers, and contexts. The context consists of both the external environment and the changing objectives that a group seeks in a particular situation. As we have seen, the traits that are most relevant to effective leadership depend on the context, and the situation creates followers' needs that lead them to search for particular leaders. A group of workers that wants someone to organize a weekend party may turn to a fun-loving member to take the lead. The same group will probably want a very different member to lead in negotiating a benefits package with management.

Rather than think of a leader as a particular type of heroic individual, we need to think of all three parts of the triangle together constituting the process of leadership. Leaders and followers learn roles and change roles as their perceptions of situations change. One of the key issues is for leaders and followers to understand how to expand and adapt their repertoires for different situations. They can learn to broaden their bandwidth and thus provide for a more effective leadership process in a wider range of situations. Because learning is possible, leadership studies, though not a science, is still a valid discipline.

THE STUDY OF LEADERSHIP

Despite the thousands of books and articles written on leadership, the social psychologists Richard Hackman and Ruth Wageman have concluded that "the field of leadership remains curiously unformed. . . . There are no generally accepted definitions of what leadership is, no dominant paradigms for studying it, and little agreement about the best strategies for developing and exercising it."[65] An article in the *Harvard Business Review* observed, "During the past 50 years, leadership scholars have conducted more than 1,000 studies in an attempt to determine the definitive styles, characteristics, or personality traits of great leaders. None of these studies has produced a clear profile of the ideal leader. Thank Goodness. If scholars had produced a cookie-cutter leadership style, individuals would be forever trying to imitate it."[66] This, of course, has not stopped myriad authors from offering popular bromides about the magical key to leadership success, usually in the business press. Some approaches are useful; most are not.

Serious scientific leadership studies have gone through several phases. The *trait-centered* approach dominated the scene up to the late 1940s, but scholars found it impossible to identify traits that predicted leadership under all conditions. When it became clear that studies of traits were indeterminate, scholars turned to a *style* approach that used questionnaires to determine how leaders behave in terms of their consideration for their followers. This held sway until the late 1960s, when it was found to be plagued with measurement problems and inconsistent results in predicting effectiveness. A new *contingency* approach was popular from the late 1960s to the early 1980s. It distinguished people-oriented from task-oriented leaders and tried to relate their performance to their degree of situational control, but this too was plagued by measurement problems and inconsistent results. It turned out that "what counts as a 'situation' and what counts as the 'appropriate' way of leading in that situation are interpretive and contestable issues, not issues that can be decided by objective criteria."[67] A new leadership approach that focuses on *charismatic and transformational* leadership has been the dominant paradigm since the early 1980s.[68] It has generated a number of useful studies, but as we will see in chapter 3, it is also plagued with definitional and empirical problems. Other useful approaches have focused on dispersed leadership, teams, and the relation of leadership to culture.

As for methods, quantitative research has been dominant. Such studies can illuminate important aspects and details of leadership behavior, but they are often limited in the scope of the generalizations they can provide. Some studies are carried out as lab experiments, often with a captive student audience. Others rest on questionnaires and surveys within the bounds of particular organizations that have established procedures and formal leadership structures. They rest heavily on the disciplinary methods of psychology and organizational behavior. But it is not clear how much these studies illuminate about political and social leadership behavior that ranges from street gangs to social movements to corporate and national presidencies. As the Oxford leadership expert Keith Grint summarizes, "The results are often informative but not definitive. The major problem seems to me to be the very complexity of the subject. There are so many potentially significant variables in establishing what counts as successful leadership that it is practically impossible to construct an effective experiment that might generate conclusive evidence on the topic."[69]

In open social situations, there are too many variables to control to be able to derive good predictive results. Science can say interesting things about aspects of leadership, but it is unlikely there will ever be a predictive science of leadership. As Richard Hackman concluded from his study of leadership in teams, humans interact in open rather than deterministic systems, and open systems behave according to a principle of "equifinality." That simply means there are different ways to behave and still achieve the same outcome.[70] A study of leadership of self-organizing social movements on the Internet found differences from leadership in other social movements but "multiple paths to leadership" on the Internet itself.[71] There are many roads to Rome, and it is often hard to predict which one will be chosen and prove effective in getting us there.

This indeterminacy and contingency has led many observers to say that leadership is an art rather than a science. The right leadership depends on the situation. The ability to mobilize a group effectively is certainly an art rather than a predictive science and varies with situations, but that does not mean that it cannot be profitably studied and learned. As Grint observes, "It would be strange if leadership was the only human skill that could not be enhanced through understanding and practice."[72] Music and painting are based in part on innate skills but also on training and practice; artists can benefit not merely from studio courses but also from art appreciation courses that introduce them to the full repertoires and palates of past masters.

Learning how to lead occurs in a variety of ways. Learning from experience is the most common and most powerful. It produces the tacit knowledge that is crucial in a crisis. But experience and intuition can be supplemented by analytics, which is the purpose of this book. As Mark Twain once observed, a cat that sits on a hot stove will not sit on a hot stove again, but it won't sit on a cold one either. Learning to analyze situations and contexts is an important leadership skill. The U.S. Army categorizes leadership learning under three words: "Be, know, do." "Be" refers to the shaping of character and values, which comes partly from training and partly from experience. "Know" refers to analysis and skills, which can be trained. "Do" refers to action and requires both training and fieldwork. Most important, however, is experience and the emphasis on learning from mistakes and a continuous process that results from what the military calls "after-action reviews."[73]

Learning can also occur in the classroom, whether through case studies, historical and analytic approaches, or experiential teaching that creates situations in the classroom that train students to increase self-awareness, to distinguish their role from their self, and to use their self as a barometer for understanding a larger group.[74]

Similarly, those interested in leadership learn from personal experience, but they can also benefit from understanding both the results of scientific studies, limited though they may be, as well as the range of behaviors that can be illuminated by historical cases and the importance of different contexts. To say something is an art rather than a science does not mean it cannot be profitably studied. And because leadership is a relationship of power, that is where we start in the next chapter.

TWO

Leadership and Power

You cannot lead if you do not have power. We use the word every day, and seldom enter a room or join a group without sensing its power relations. Nonetheless, power is hard to measure.[1] But that is also true of love, and we do not doubt its reality simply because we cannot say we love someone 1.7 times more than someone else. Like love (and leadership), power is a relationship whose strength and domain will vary with different contexts. Those with more power in a relationship are better placed to make and resist change.[2] Empirical studies have shown that the more powerful are less likely to take on the perspectives of others.[3]

The dictionary tells us that power is the ability to affect the behavior of others to get the outcomes you want. You can do that in three main ways: you can coerce them with threats, you can induce them with payments, or you can attract or co-opt them.

Some people think of power narrowly in terms of command and coercion. They imagine that power consists solely of commanding others to do what they would otherwise not do.[4] You say "Jump," and they jump. This appears to be a simple test of power, but it is not so straightforward. Suppose, like my granddaughters, they already wanted to jump. When we view power in terms of the changed behavior of others, we first have to know their preferences. What would have happened without the command? A cruel dictator can lock up or execute a dissident, but that may not prove his power if the dissenter was really seeking martyrdom. And the power may evaporate when the context (including your objectives) changes. A tough boss who controls your behavior at work has no power over how you raise your daughter (although others outside your family, such as a doctor, may have such influence). The domain of your boss's power in this case is limited to work. Power always depends on the context of the relationship.[5]

Sometimes people define power as the possession of resources that can influence outcomes. A person or group is powerful if it is large, stable, and wealthy. This approach makes power appear concrete and measurable, but it is mistaken because it confuses the results of a power relationship with the means to that end. Some analysts call this the "vehicle fallacy" or the "concrete fallacy." It treats power as something concrete that you can drop on your foot or on a city. But such concrete vehicles as bombs and bullets may not produce the outcomes you want. People defining power as synonymous with the resources that produce it sometimes encounter the paradox that those best endowed with power resources do not always get the behavioral outcomes they want. After all, the United States lost the Vietnam War to a weaker and more determined opponent, and the richest politicians do not always win the elections. A player holding the highest cards can still lose the game.

SOFT POWER

Police power, financial power, and the ability to hire and fire are examples of tangible, *hard* power that can be used to get others to change their position. Hard power rests on inducements (carrots) and threats (sticks). But sometimes one can get the outcomes one wants by setting the agenda and attracting others without threat or payment. This is *soft* power: getting the outcomes one wants by attracting others rather than manipulating their material incentives. It co-opts people rather than coerces them.[6]

Soft power rests on the ability to shape the preferences of others to want what you want. At the personal level, we all know the power of attraction and seduction. Power in a relationship or a marriage does not necessarily reside with the larger partner. Smart executives know that leadership is not just a matter of issuing commands, but also involves leading by example and attracting others to do what you want them to do. It is difficult to run a large organization by commands alone unless you can get others to buy in to your values. As one business expert comments, "Managers can't control everything. They must instead work through influence, persuasion and an awful lot of training. And corporate culture—the common organizational values that people learn—is often what guides people, not the rules or the instructions of any one manager."[7]

Community-based police work relies on making the police friendly and attractive enough that a community wants to help them achieve their shared objectives. Military theories of counterinsurgency stress the importance of winning the hearts and minds of the population, not merely killing the enemy. Similarly, political leaders have long understood the power that comes from setting the agenda and determining the framework of a debate.

While leaders in authoritarian countries can use coercion and issue commands, politicians in democracies must rely more on a combination of inducement and attraction. Soft power is a staple of daily democratic politics. Even in the military, attraction and commitment play an important role. As the former army chief of staff Eric Shinseki put it, "You can certainly command without that sense of commitment, but you cannot lead without it. And without leadership, command is a hollow experience, a vacuum often filled with mistrust and arrogance."[8]

Of course, in many real-world situations, people's motives are mixed. Moreover, the distinction between hard and soft power is one of degree, both in the nature of the behavior and in the tangibility of the resources. Both are aspects of the ability to achieve one's purposes by affecting the behavior of others. Command power—the ability to change what others do—can rest on coercion or inducement. Co-optive power—the ability to shape what others want—can rest on the attractiveness of one's values or the ability to set the agenda of political choices. In real-world situations, hard and soft power are often combined, sometimes with a soft layer of attraction overlaid on underlying relationships that rest on coercion or payment.[9] A lobbyist may first try to persuade a legislator, but the lobbyist may also make a legal and well-timed campaign contribution. A government may try to persuade young people to forgo drugs with an advertisement campaign featuring attractive celebrities, but if this soft power fails, the hard power of law enforcement remains.

The ability to establish preferences tends to follow from often intangible assets such as an attractive personality, culture, values, and moral authority. If I can attract you to want to do what I want you to do, then I do not have to force you to do what you do *not* want to do. If a leader represents values that others want to follow, it will cost less to lead. Soft power allows the leader to save on carrots and sticks. For example, loyal Catholics may follow the pope's teaching on capital punishment not because of a threat of excommunication, but out of respect for his moral authority. Some radical Muslims are attracted to support Osama bin Laden's actions not because of payments or threats, but because they believe in the legitimacy of his objectives. Even after bin Laden's organization was disrupted by the U.S. military presence in Afghanistan, many terrorist groups around the world organized themselves in his image.

Soft power is not merely the same as influence, though it is one source of influence. After all, influence can also rest on the hard power of threats or payments.[10] Nor is soft power just persuasion or the ability to move people by argument, though that is an important part of it. It is also the ability to entice and attract. Attraction often leads to acquiescence. In behavioral terms, soft power is attractive power. In terms of resources, soft power resources are the assets—tangible and intangible—that produce such attraction.

People's decisions in the marketplace of ideas are often shaped by an intangible attraction that persuades them to go along with others' purposes without any explicit exchange of tangible threats or rewards taking place. Soft power uses a different currency (not force, not money) to engender cooperation. It can rest on a sense of attraction, love, or duty in a relationship, and appeal to values about the justness of contributing to those shared values and purposes.[11]

Soft power can provide what fund-raisers call "the power of the ask." Someone calls and asks you to make a donation. Sometimes you say yes because it is a good cause or in an exchange of favors, but sometimes you do so simply because of the moral authority of the person asking. In a nonprofit organization, the leader may ask you to undertake a task; you say yes not because the leader can threaten or pay you, but simply because of who he or she is. An index of leaders' power is the frequency, size, and range of requests they can successfully make of you. In institutions with flat hierarchies like universities and other nonprofit organizations, soft power is often the major asset available to a leader.[12] Once that soft power has eroded, little else is left. People just say no. Even in the U.S. presidency, as the political scientist Richard Neustadt argued, power is mostly the ability to persuade others that they want to do in their own interests what you want them to do.[13] As Dwight Eisenhower put the case for soft power, leadership is an ability "to get people to work together, not only because you tell them to do so and enforce your orders but because they instinctively want to do it for you. . . . You don't lead by hitting people over the head; that's assault, not leadership."[14]

THE POWER OF FOLLOWERS

Why do people follow at all? In ordinary circumstances they have functional needs for meaning, group identity and cohesion, order, and the ability to get work accomplished. Leaders fill these needs by a combination of fear, payment, and attraction—hard and soft power. In some circumstances, people have deep personality needs and develop a culture of permissiveness that transfers enormous hard and soft power to a leader. In 1978 in Guyana, Jim Jones persuaded more than nine hundred members of his Peoples Temple to commit mass suicide rather than face the dissolution of his cult.[15] In 1945, as Soviet troops closed in on Hitler's bunker in Berlin, Joseph Goebbels and his wife killed their children rather than have them face a world without their führer.[16]

In times of social crisis, such as war or economic depression, temporarily overwhelmed followers may hand over power to leaders, which later they find difficult to retrieve. Hitler came to power by election in Germany in 1933 and then used coercion to consolidate his power. But he also used the soft power of attraction, constructing narratives that turned Jews into scapegoats, glorified the past, and promised a thousand-year Reich as a vision of the future. Followers also helped to create Hitler. As Albert Speer, one of Hitler's acolytes, put it, "Of course Goebbels and Hitler know how to penetrate through to the instincts of their audience; but in a deeper sense they derived their whole existence from the audience. Certainly the masses roared to the beat set by Hitler and Goebbels's baton; yet they were not the true conductors. The mob determined the theme."[17]

One can think of Hitler's followers in terms of concentric circles, with true believers like Goebbels, Göring, and Speer as an inner core; they are followed by a circle of "good soldiers" like the Hamburg Reserve Police Battalion 101, who, in a show of "crushing conformity," willingly executed Jews and Poles;[18] an outer circle of complicit bystanders who knowingly acquiesced; and a further circle of passive bystanders who made no effort to know what was behind the myths and propaganda. Beyond them were those who refused to follow and resisted, many of whom were killed or coerced into silence.[19]

Similar circles existed in other totalitarian systems, such as Stalin's Soviet Union and Mao's China. Even before the advent of modern totalitarianism, for thousands of years most people lived under authoritarian political regimes. This does not mean that they were totally powerless. Peasants, workers, and religious and ethnic groups have occasionally revolted, sometimes with success. Kings have been killed. But resistance and rebellion are costly, and most subordinates lack the necessary means to succeed. Even when they appear to be docile, however, such subordinates may rebel continuously through withholding effort or quiet sabotage of leaders' orders.[20] Even ostensibly powerless followers may retain a degree of power over the ability of leaders to accomplish their ends.

Some discussions of leadership treat followers as obedient sheep. Followers can be defined by their *position* as subordinates or by their *behavior* of going along with leaders' wishes. But subordinates do not always go along fully with leaders' wishes. Leadership, like power, is a relationship, and followers also have power both to resist and to lead. Followers empower leaders as well as vice versa. This has led some leadership analysts like Ronald Heifetz to avoid using the word "followers" and refer to the others in a power relationship as citizens or constituents.[21]

Heifetz is correct that too simple a view of followers can produce misunderstanding. In modern life, most people wind up being both leaders and followers, and the categories can become quite fluid. Our behavior as followers changes as our objectives change. If I trust your judgment in music more than my own, I may follow your lead on which concert we attend (even though you may be formally my subordinate in position). But if I am an expert on fishing, you may follow my lead on where we fish, regardless of our formal positions or the fact that I followed your lead on concerts yesterday.

Regardless of what positions they hold in a group, followers' behavior can be ranked by its intensity and sorted into categories, such as alienated, exemplary, conformist, passive, and pragmatic.[22] And followers' behavior may fit one category on some issues and another category on other issues. For example, a Republican who is an exemplary supporter of the president on social and fiscal issues may be alienated over the Iraq War. Types of follower behavior vary with the cultural homogeneity, agreement on basic values, and fragmentation over issues that exist in groups and societies. A leader may have a great deal of soft power with followers in one domain and very little in another.

Even in large organizations, where subordinates have few positional power resources, they may be able to exercise leadership. If a boss has great confidence in an assistant's judgment, she may often follow the assistant's lead. In practice, few of us occupy top positions in groups or organizations. Most people lead from the middle, attracting and persuading in both upward and downward directions. A successful middle-level leader persuades and attracts his boss as well as his subordinates. Richard Haass, who served in several American administrations, uses the metaphor of a compass: "North represents those for whom you work. To the South are those who work for you. East stands for colleagues, those in your organization with whom you work. West represents those outside your organization who have the potential to affect matters that affect you."[23] Effective leadership from the middle often requires leading in all directions of that compass.

Lee Iacocca was a successful executive at Ford Motor Company in the 1980s with great skills at managing the press and was widely regarded as a leader, but not in all directions. "Although Iacocca's self promotion had a favorable impact on his perception as a leader, it had negative effects as well. Iacocca's increasing recognition as 'the' leader of Ford Motor Company soured his long-standing relationship with Henry Ford (chairman of the board), a situation that was the major factor in his dismissal." His successor, Philip Caldwell, "stressed the importance of everyone's (management's, union workers', and key suppliers') contribution," but he received less public recognition as the leader who turned the company's performance around.[24] Leaders in the middle who forget to attract and persuade in all directions often cease to be leaders.

Whatever they are called, there are no leaders without followers, and followers often initiate group activities. In the possibly apocryphal words of the French revolutionary Comte de Mirabeau, "There goes the mob, and I must follow them, for I am their leader."[25] More seriously, good leaders commonly intuit where their "followers" are trending and adjust accordingly. Followers often have the power to help lead a group. After his New Deal slowed down in the mid-1930s, Franklin Roosevelt reinitiated his legislative programs in response to pressures from new political and social movements in the country.[26] We saw in the previous chapter that in many groups and organizations, leaders and followers are interchangeable in different situations, and both goals and initiatives can originate among followers.

Even when they do not take initiative, followers have the power to set constraints on leaders. In the hunter–gatherer societies discussed earlier, followers use ridicule, secession, ostracism, and even assassination to limit leaders who try to claim more power than their followers are willing to grant.[27] Modern liberal democracies constrain leaders with constitutions, laws, and norms. In open source software Internet communities, members develop a culture that limits the effective authority of leaders, and those exceeding such limits lose their followers.[28] They just log off.

The power of leaders depends on the followers' objectives that are embedded in their culture. For example, George Washington was an exemplary leader who is often credited with establishing the American republic by refusing a monarchical role. Followers lavished adulation upon him and he was revered as a demigod; his image was everywhere. In exalting Washington, the new Americans exalted their cause, and Washington became the symbol of the nation. He had great soft power, but that power was limited not only by the institutions of Congress and courts but also by a political culture that was hostile to the exercise of authority. "Washington's great prestige did not provide the foundation for him to become a more dominant political figure because of the ambivalent attitudes Americans had (and have) toward political leaders. The very fact that he was so highly esteemed also made Washington the object of enormous suspicion."[29] Having fought themselves free of one King George, Washington's followers were determined not to allow another.

If leaders of a dominant culture are able to prevent people from having or covertly expressing grievances by completely shaping their worldviews and preferences, then followers have little power.[30] However, such extreme degrees of control are rare. Totalitarian governments have often tried to make subordinates accept their role in the existing order of things through a combination of hard coercive power and an ideological version of soft power, but with only partial success. Even in Stalin's Russia, Hitler's Germany, and Mao's China, it proved difficult to completely overcome all followers' covert forms of resistance. Moreover, in most instances, the power relationship between leaders and followers is far from so one-sided.

THE MIXTURE OF HARD AND SOFT POWER

A century ago, in asking why people follow or obey, the great German sociologist Max Weber identified three ideal types of authority or legitimated power.[31] Two depend on position and one on person. Under traditional authority, a person follows another because the latter is chief or king or emperor by right of some traditional process such as heredity. Under rational or legal authority, a person follows because the other is president or director or chair and has been properly elected or appointed based on rational criteria. Under charismatic authority, a person follows another because the latter embodies a gift of grace or exceptional magnetism. In the first two instances, followers obey because of the power of the position, in the last case because of the power of the person.

The distinction between informal personal power and power that grows out of a formal position is not exactly the same as the distinction between hard and soft power.[32] Some leaders without formal authority, such as gang leaders, may effectively use coercion as well as charisma, and some military officers have the soft power of charisma as well as the hard power conveyed by their position. Moreover, certain formal positions such as pope and president extract obedience from followers who are attracted by the legitimacy of the institution even if the incumbent has very little personal appeal. But generally, those without formal authority tend to rely more on soft power, whereas those in formal positions are better placed to mix hard and soft power resources. Social movements tend to be volatile and complex formations devoted to causes like civil rights, women's liberation, or environmental issues, and they rarely have clear and stable structures; usually their hierarchies are flat or nonexistent. With few material incentives under their control, leaders of social movements have few hard power resources and tend to rely on soft power and inspirational style.[33]

Even with authority and structure, however, hard and soft power resources can change over time. As Heifetz points out, "The formal powers of the President of the United States rarely change during a four year term, but the real power to govern fluctuates weekly as the President's informal authority—approval rating, professional respect, moral standing—waxes and wanes."[34] For example, in 2007, Republican Senator Jeff Sessions of Alabama described the problems of the Bush administration this way: "When you are first elected, you have some momentum and you have more ability to persuade. In the last months of any administration, getting people to do something simply because the president asks for it is less. That's certainly true here."[35] The position remains the same, but the personal power changes.

There are various types of personal attraction. People are drawn to others both by their inherent qualities and by the effect of their communications. The emotional or magnetic quality of inherent attraction is often called charisma, and we will look at it more closely in the next chapter. Communications can be symbolic (leadership by example) or by persuasion, for example, arguments and visions that cause others to believe, respect, trust, and follow. When such persuasion has a large component of emotion as well as reason, we call it rhetoric. Some communications are designed to limit reasoning and frame issues as impractical or illegitimate in such a way that they never get on the agenda for real discussion.[36] During periods of insecurity, leaders may appeal to patriotic rhetoric to exclude criticism from the public discussion. At this point, persuasion blurs into propaganda and indoctrination.

As for hard power, threats and inducements are closely related. Inducements, rewards, and bonuses are more pleasant to receive than threats, but the hint of their removal can constitute an effective threat.[37] If I can pay you a bonus, I can also threaten to take away your bonus. Some economists argue that there is no power relationship in freely struck market bargains; if you do not like the terms on offer, you can just walk away. But that assumes equal resources and equal needs. If I depend on you more than you depend on me, you have power. Asymmetry in interdependent relationships provides power to the less dependent party.[38] These types of power are summarized in Table 2.1.

Hard and soft power are related because they are both approaches to achieving one's purpose by affecting the behavior of others. Sometimes people are attracted to others with command power by myths of invincibility. In some extreme cases, known as "the Stockholm syndrome," fearful hostages become attracted to their captors. Adam Smith noted in his *Theory of Moral Sentiments* more than two centuries ago, "We see frequently the vices and follies of the powerful much less despised than the poverty and weakness of the innocent."[39] Or, as Osama bin Laden put it more

TABLE 2.1 Soft and Hard Power

Type of Power	Behavior	Sources	Examples
Soft	Attract and co-opt	Inherent qualities	Charisma
		Communications	Persuasion, rhetoric, example
Hard	Threaten and induce	Threats and intimidation	Hire, fire, and demote
		Payments and rewards	Promotions and compensation

recently in one of his videos, "When people see a strong horse and a weak horse, by nature, they will like the strong horse."[40]

Among the great industrial titans, Andrew Carnegie of Carnegie Steel Corporation and Thomas J. Watson of IBM led primarily by intimidation; George Eastman of Kodak and Robert Noyce of Intel led primarily through inspiration.[41] Sometimes intimidators have a vision, belief in their cause, and a reputation for success that attracts others despite their bullying behavior— witness the examples of Steve Jobs, Martha Stewart, and Hyman Rickover, the father of the nuclear navy.[42] Rickover was a small man, far from the top of his class at Annapolis, who did not look the part of a warrior or swashbuckling sea captain. His success as a navy leader came from his bureaucratic skills in cultivating congressional support and resources and from a rigid discipline that tolerated no failures among his officers. The result was the creation of an efficient and accident-free nuclear submarine force that developed a mystique of success that attracted bright young officers. Able people wanted to join him because Rickover was renowned for implementing an important strategic vision, not because he was a nice boss.[43]

Although some studies suggest that bullying is detrimental to organizational performance,[44] the Stanford psychologist Roderick Kramer argues that bullies who have a vision and disdain social constraints are "great intimidators" who often succeed. As a Silicon Valley venture capitalist once told me, "Almost all our great innovators are jerks." Larry Ellison, Steve Jobs, and Bill Gates are not known for their soft touch. Similarly in politics, the British Conservative leader John Major was a much nicer person than Margaret Thatcher, but Chris Patten (who served as a minister under both) reports that her bullying made her a more effective prime minister.[45] Machiavelli famously said that it is more important for a prince to be feared than to be loved. And while some studies report that Machiavellianism (defined as manipulative, exploitive, and deceitful behavior) is negatively correlated with leadership performance, other studies have found a positive relationship.[46] So where does leadership theory now stand on the roles of hard and soft power?

Hard and soft power sometimes reinforce and sometimes interfere with each other. Although Jim Jones used soft power to persuade his followers to commit mass suicide, he had an inner core of about eight henchmen who used a degree of coercion on followers who threatened to defect. Growing awareness of this use of hard power threatened to pop the bubble of the cult's illusions and accelerated its sad end. In responding to Al Qaeda's terrorist attacks on the United States, Vice President Dick Cheney argued that a strong military response would deter further attacks. Certainly the hard power of military and police force was necessary to counter Al Qaeda, but the indiscriminate use of hard power illustrated by the invasion of Iraq, the Abu Ghraib prison pictures, and the Guantánamo detentions without trial served to increase the number of terrorist recruits (according to official British and U.S. intelligence estimates).[47] The absence of an effective soft power component undercut the strategy to respond to terrorism.

Almost every leader needs a certain degree of soft power. The leadership theorist James MacGregor Burns once argued that those who rely on coercion are not leaders but mere power wielders: "A leader and a tyrant are polar opposites."[48] Thus in his view, Hitler was not a leader. Burns is correct that not all power behavior is leadership, but even tyrants and despots such as Hitler need to have a degree of soft power, at least within an inner circle. As David Hume pointed out more than two centuries ago, no individual alone is strong enough to coerce everyone else.[49] A dictator must attract or induce an inner circle of henchmen to impose his coercive techniques on others. Such masters of coercion as Hitler, Stalin, and Mao attracted and relied on acolytes.

Except for some religious leaders, such as the Dalai Lama, who combines personal and positional power, soft power is rarely sufficient. And a leader who only courts popularity may be reluctant to exercise hard power when he or she should. Alternatively, leaders who throw their weight around without regard to the effects on their soft power may find others placing obstacles in the way of their hard power. Psychologists have found that too much assertiveness by a leader worsens relationships, just as too little limits achievement: "Like salt in a sauce, too much overwhelms the dish; too little is similarly distracting; but just the right amount allows the other flavors to dominate our experience."[50] In the words of CEO Jeff Immelt, "When you run General Electric, there are 7 to 12 times a year when you have to say, 'you're doing it my way.' If you do it 18 times, the good people will leave. If you do it 3 times, the company falls apart."[51]

Machiavelli may be correct that it is better for a prince to be feared than to be loved, but we sometimes forget that the opposite of love is not fear, but hatred. And Machiavelli made it clear that hatred is something a prince should carefully avoid.[52] When the exercise of hard power undercuts soft power, it makes leadership more difficult—as President Bush found out after the invasion of Iraq. The ability to combine hard and soft power into an effective strategy is *smart power*.

Soft power is not good per se, and it is not always better than hard power. Nobody likes to feel manipulated, even by soft power. Soft power can be used for competitive purposes, and we often talk about wars of words: one person's attraction pitted against another's. A president may campaign against legislators in their home districts or run television ads pushing his agenda and attacking theirs. He is using his attraction to combat theirs and thus putting pressure on them. In that sense, soft power can feel coercive, but it is a very different sense of coercion than what the victim experiences with physical (though not economic) hard power. In a competition with soft power, it matters very much what you and others think. If I shoot you to achieve my objective, it does not matter much what you think.

Like any form of power, soft power can be wielded for good or bad purposes, and these often vary according to the eye of the beholder. Bin Laden possesses a great deal of soft power in the eyes of his followers, but that does not make his actions good from an outside point of view. It is not necessarily better to twist minds than to twist arms. If I want to steal your money, I can threaten you with a gun, I can lure you into a fraudulent get-rich-quick scheme, or I can persuade you with a false claim that I am a guru who will save the world. I can then abscond with your money. The first two approaches rest on the hard power of coercion and inducement, whereas the third depends solely on attraction or soft power. Nonetheless, the intentions and result remain theft in all three instances. On the other hand, soft power uses means that allow (on the surface, at least) more choice and leeway to the victim than hard power does. The views and choices of followers matter more in the case of soft power. We will return to these questions in the final chapter, about good and bad leadership.

POWER AND NETWORKS

Long-term trends in the economy and society such as globalization and the information revolution are increasing the importance of networks and changing the context of leadership. Globalization simply means networks of interdependence at intercontinental distances, and it is as old as human history. Early migrations of humans out of Africa populated the empty continents; the silk route connected Asia with medieval Europe; the world economy was more integrated in 1914 than it was again until 1970. What is new today is that global networks are quicker and thicker. As the columnist Thomas Friedman and others have observed, in today's "flat world," geographical distance no longer protects against competition and threats as well as it once did.[53] That poses new problems for business and national leaders.

In a world of cell phones, computers, and websites such as MySpace, Facebook, and LinkedIn, it is commonplace to say that we increasingly live in a networked world. Networks build social capital that leaders can draw on to get things done. Networks are relationships, and different types of networks provide different forms of power. An airline hub and spokes, a spider web, a bus route, an electricity grid, and the Internet are all networks, though they vary in terms of centralization and the complexity of connections. Centrality in networks can convey power, particularly where there are "structural holes."[54] Think of the hub and spokes of a wheel; if there is no rim connecting the spokes to each other, structural holes exist and the hub gains power from being the central node of communication. As Sir Francis Bacon observed four centuries ago, knowledge is power, and in today's information age, the control of information flows in networks is an important source of power for leaders. So also is the ability to process vast, diverse flows so that the information becomes knowledge and not mere noise.[55]

Some networks have strong ties in terms of frequency and reciprocity of contacts, and others have weak ties.[56] Think of the difference between friendships and acquaintances. Valuable information is more likely to be shared by friends than among acquaintances. But weak ties that reach out further may provide more novel information. Networks based on strong ties have the power of loyalty but may become cliques that merely recirculate the conventional wisdom in a group; they may succumb to groupthink. Weak ties are more effective than strong ties for acquiring novel, innovative, and nonredundant information. Strong ties may provide the power of loyalty but be resistant to change; weak ties may provide "the necessary information and ability to link diverse groups together in a cooperative, successful manner."[57] Democratic leadership rests upon such strategies. Such weak networks are part of the glue that holds diverse societies together. A great democratic politician has to be a person with a great capacity for shallow friendships. Leaders will increasingly need to understand the relationship of networks to power and how to adapt strategies and create teams that benefit from both strong and weak ties.

One of the open questions about networks is the effect of the Internet on future leadership styles. In the absence of face-to-face cues, verbal persuasion should become more important, but the study of leadership online is still in its infancy. Will younger generations who spend large parts of their lives in networks that are marked by physical separation and virtual connection have different attitudes about leadership? Some early studies suggest that adolescents may be constructing their own styles of leadership and community involvement, with greater emphasis on cooperation, sociability, and soft power. One study of adolescents finds that success in becoming a leader in the online world is less dependent on age and gender than in the offline world and more determined by linguistic skills and the quantity of talk.[58]

Equally interesting for the question of leadership is what globalization is doing to the group question "Who is us?" Beyond a small scale, all human groups and identities are "imagined communities."[59] No one can know everyone else, and leaders' roles in shaping myths of group identity become increasingly complicated when more than half of a company's employees live outside its native country, cheap transportation keeps diaspora communities closely connected across national boundaries, and the Internet allows professional, ethnic, religious, terrorist, and other groups to create transnational communities. Humans have always been capable of multiple identities, but traditionally they took the form of concentric circles that tended to weaken with distance. Prior to August 1914, transnational networks of bankers, labor unions, and socialist movements crisscrossed Europe, but they succumbed to the nation-state, collapsing under the demands of national loyalty that overwhelmed them after World War I commenced.

In today's global world, a better metaphor might be networks of Venn diagrams. (Think of the overlapping circles that are produced when you set a cold beer bottle down on a dry table top several times.) In such overlapping circles, some identities become intermixed and hard to separate. This raises interesting puzzles for leaders of such networks. Leaders are identity entrepreneurs who increase their power by activating and mobilizing some of their followers' multiple identities at the cost of others. In today's world, national identity usually prevails, but how insular should leaders be in responding to other groups' needs? What about conflicting loyalties when groups overlap? This all seems quite abstract until one looks at how leaders have struggled to respond to cases of genocide such as in Rwanda and Darfur. Intergroup leadership becomes more complex and more important.[60] We will return to the ethical questions raised by these issues in the final chapter.

The other major change in the macrocontext of leadership is the information revolution, which is simply the dramatic drop in the costs of computing and communication. For instance, the cost of computing dropped a thousand-fold between 1970 and 2000. If the price of automobiles had dropped that rapidly, you could buy a car today for $5. With such a dramatic drop in costs, the barriers to entry into markets and politics are lowered and more players enter the game. In 1970, instantaneous global communication was possible but expensive, and thus restricted to large hierarchical organizations with big budgets like governments and multinational corporations. Today, anyone with a few dollars can enter an Internet café and have the same communication power that was once reserved for the rich. This has empowered many more actors to be involved in political life. Nonprofit groups devoted to the environment or human rights such as Greenpeace or Amnesty International are better placed to challenge governments or launch boycotts against vulnerable corporate brands. Transnational terrorists have also found the Internet to be a particularly powerful tool in recruiting, training, and sending instructions across borders.

If information can create power, it is important to realize that more people have more information today than at any time in human history. Technology democratizes social and political processes and, for better and worse, institutions play less of a mediating role. When a politician makes a mistake, such as George

Allen's use of the word "macaca" to refer to a dark-skinned supporter of his opponent in Virginia's 2006 senatorial campaign,
millions of people see it on YouTube within days. In fact, the basic
concept of Web 2.0 on the Internet rests on the concept of user-
based content bubbling up from the bottom rather than des-
cending from the top of a traditional hierarchy of information.
Institutions like Wikipedia and Linux are examples of social production that involve very different roles for leaders than do their
traditional counterparts, *Encyclopaedia Britannica* and Microsoft.

The information revolution is affecting the structure of organizations. Hierarchies are becoming flatter and embedded in fluid
networks of contacts. White-collar knowledge workers respond
to different incentives and political appeals than do blue-collar
industrial workers.[61] Polls show that people today are less deferential to authority in organizations and politics.

In 1930, the Nobel Prize–winning economist Ronald Coase
tried to explain the rise of the modern corporation. Why not just
rely on markets? His answer was transactions costs: anonymous
partners were hard to identify, contracts were difficult to manage,
and it was more reliable to produce supplies yourself than to count
on external networks of suppliers. Today cheap and reliable information makes networks of outsourcing more attractive. The
classic economic theory of the firm as a hierarchical organization
that internalizes functions in order to reduce transactions costs
(think GM) is being supplemented by the notion of firms as networks of outsourcing (think Toyota or Nike). According to the
Financial Times, "More companies now consist essentially of intangible assets such as patents plus the values embedded in their
brands. In a flatter world, the advantages of innovation do not last
as long and there are fewer things sheltering companies from
competition. . . . The proportion of intangible assets to shareholder

value at Fortune 500 companies has steadily risen from about 50 per cent in 1980 to 70 per cent today."[62]

In some cases, one can orchestrate a complex network simply with carefully specified contracts, but the friction of normal life usually creates ambiguities that cannot be fully met in advance. In describing the success of the Toyota and the Linux networks, Philip Evans and Bob Wolf of Boston Consulting Group conclude, "Monetary carrots and accountability sticks motivate people to perform narrow, specified tasks. Admiration and applause are far more effective stimulants of above and beyond behavior."[63] Traditional business leadership styles become less effective, but some new styles seem bizarre. Visitors to the headquarters of a Web 2.0 company in Silicon Valley would be forgiven if they thought they had entered a nursery school playroom rather than a corporate office.

According to Samuel J. Palmisano, CEO of IBM, under these new conditions "hierarchical, command-and-control approaches simply do not work anymore. They impede information flows inside companies, hampering the fluid and collaborative nature of work today."[64] A study of a major bricks-and-clicks company (one that combines offline and online operations) found that distributive leadership was essential: "In dynamic, complex, and ambiguous contexts like the dotcom environment, the traditional view of a leader's being decisively in control is difficult to reconcile. ... Effective leadership depends on the use of multiple 'leaders' for capable decision-making and action-taking."[65] Harvard Business School professor John Quelch writes that "business success increasingly depends on the subtleties of soft power."[66] Management gurus refer to "level 5" and "authentic" leadership that is more collaborative and integrative.[67] One management expert summarized twenty-five years of recent studies this way: "We have observed an increase in the use of more participative processes."[68]

Politics and government are changing as well. Polls show that people today have become less deferential to authority in public institutions and in politics. Levels of trust in large institutions have declined in nearly all advanced countries.[69] The way that governments work is also changing. They are constructing and using market mechanisms for public purposes. Like firms, they are doing more outsourcing and contracting rather than production. More effort goes into negotiating and managing networks of public and private actors. Government work involves less direct production and more indirect regulation. Governments enter more public-private partnerships. To use a crew metaphor, governments do less rowing and more steering than in the past.[70] For example, in a new model of leadership, the Environmental Protection Agency now devotes significant resources to developing regulations in collaboration with its various stakeholders.[71] Success in managing such public and private networks depends on "talent, trust and soft power."[72] In short, new conditions require a new style of public leadership.

Some say these new conditions mean that leaders are finally entering a woman's world, but such stereotypes do not capture the full complexity of the change that is occurring. Postheroic leadership "depends less on the heroic actions of a few individuals at the top and more on collaborative leadership practices distributed throughout an organization."[73] Women are said to have a greater ability to work networks, to collaborate, and to nurture. Their nonhierarchical style and relational skills fill a leadership gap in the new world of knowledge-based organizations and groups that men are less well prepared to fill. According to one influential article, "Women leaders don't covet formal authority. They have learned to lead without it."[74]

In the past, in terms of gender stereotypes, when women fought their way to the top of organizations they often had to adopt a "masculine style," violating the broader social norm of female "niceness," and they were often punished for it. In the new view, with the information revolution and democratization demanding more participatory and integrative leadership, the "feminine style" is becoming a path to more effective leadership. Various social scientific analyses of leadership and gender confirm the increased success of what was once considered a "feminine style of leadership."[75] Nonetheless, women lag in leadership positions, holding only 5 percent of top corporate positions and a minority of positions in elected legislatures (ranging from 45 percent in Sweden to 16 percent in the United States). One study of the 1,941 rulers of independent countries throughout the twentieth century found only twenty-seven women, and half of them came to power as the widow or daughter of a male ruler; fewer than 1 percent of twentieth-century rulers were women who gained power on their own.[76] If leadership opportunities are finally opening for women, it has been a long time coming.

Gender bias, lack of experience, primary caregiver responsibilities, and bargaining style all help to explain this gender gap. The traditional career paths for women do not enable women to gain the requisite experiences for top leadership positions in most organizational contexts. Moreover, women are likely to have a harder time than men negotiating for those resources and opportunities for leadership. Research shows that even in democratic cultures, women are less effective than men at promoting their own self-interest and face a higher social risk than men when attempting to negotiate for career-related resources such as compensation.[77] Women are generally not well integrated into male networks or included in organizations' dominant coalitions.[78] In addition, broader gender stereotypes about the expression of emotions still hamper women who try to overcome such barriers.[79]

Regardless of the disconnect between the ascendance of a new softer style and continuing gender bias, there is a danger in identifying the new type of leadership in gender-stereotypical terms.[80] By using stereotypes, even positive ones, "the great man (or trait) theory of leadership is being applied to women's leadership, but at the group rather than the individual level . . . and that can be perilous for women, men and effective leadership in general."[81] As seen in the previous chapter, leadership should be seen less in heroic terms of command than as sharing and encouraging participation throughout an organization, group, or network. This is becoming increasingly true in the age of globalization and the information revolution. Some situations call for a leader with transformational objectives and an inspirational style. But questions of appropriate style—when to use hard and soft power—in a networked world are equally relevant for men and women and should not be clouded by traditional gender stereotypes. We turn to these questions of leadership style in the next chapter.

THREE

Types and Skills

Leaders come in a great variety of sizes, shapes, and types. To survey them all would accomplish little. Because I am primarily interested in the types and skills of leaders that are relevant to modern democratic societies and organizations, I will focus on the currently dominant theoretical approach, called the "neocharismatic and transformational leaders paradigm." It gives us a start on understanding contemporary leadership, but, as we shall see, the concepts need clarification.

CHARISMATIC LEADERSHIP

One of the most common ways to differentiate types of leaders is to call them charismatic or noncharismatic. Almost every journalist has used the term: this presidential candidate has charisma and another lacks it. Charisma produces soft power, for better and for worse. Some of history's best and worst leaders have been described as charismatic. Mahatma Gandhi and Adolf Hitler were both charismatic leaders in the 1930s. Martin Luther King Jr. and Alabama Governor George Wallace were each regarded as charismatic in the 1960s, though by different groups.

To take a more recent example, many people regarded British Prime Minister Tony Blair as charismatic. As a Conservative opponent described Blair at the end of a decade in office:

> What he was able to accomplish was largely due to his charisma—a rare thing in British politics, but Blair's ranks second only to Bill Clinton's. When he won power a decade ago, he told voters it was a new political dawn, and they actually believed him. . . . When later that year it fell to him to express the nation's grief over the death of Diana, the Princess of Wales, he hit exactly the right note. . . . More substantially, within a few more months he had induced the Irish Republican Army to renounce violence and he brought together politicians from across the divide. . . . Unfortunately, he is a rhetorician and not a manager. . . . At one time this undisputed master of spin could make most people believe anything. By now, it is hard to find anyone who believes a word he says.[1]

This opponent's assessment of Blair may be biased, but his recognition of charismatic power is important. It is all the more remarkable because Britons "tend to mistrust charisma."[2]

Japan is another contemporary polity that has tended not to produce charismatic leaders. In the past half-century, most Japanese prime ministers rose to power by serving loyally in one or another of the factions of the Liberal Democratic Party rather than by appealing directly to the public. Leaders arose out of bargaining among factions. In 2001, sensing public disillusion and impending electoral defeat, the party nominated Junichiro Koizumi, who then went on to surprise the Japanese by using the media to appeal directly to the public with a unique personal style. He was soon described as charismatic and used that reputation as a source of power to weaken the once all-powerful factions that had selected him, enact reforms, and ensure his reelection. His successor, however, lacked Koizumi's charisma, and Japanese politics reverted to its more traditional, behind-the-scenes process of bargaining among factions.

Abu Musab al-Zarqawi was a different type of contemporary charismatic leader. Until he was killed in Iraq in 2006, he was "a charismatic figure who was building the next generation of terrorists." A onetime street thug who grew up in Jordan, Zarqawi made a name for himself with Internet and satellite broadcasts of grisly videos and rants. But he had direct command of only a small fraction of the insurgents in Iraq. He was mostly a looming image whose contribution to the war derived from his symbolic value.[3] Though he used the hard power of coercion against U.S. troops and Iraqi Shia, his influence among the Sunni insurgents came from the soft power of his charisma, not the numbers under his command. Similarly, after 2002 Osama bin Laden's command authority over the disrupted remnants of the Al Qaeda organization diminished, but his influence grew globally because of his charisma.

In common usage, charisma is the special power of a person to inspire fascination and loyalty. Charismatic leaders are often described as self-confident, with strong convictions, high energy, enthusiasm that they communicate to others, and an ability to manipulate symbols of power and success to create an emotional attraction for followers. The word "charisma" comes from religious language, and that has left an aura of magic and mystery. *Charisma* is the Greek word for "divine gift" or "gift of grace."

As we saw in chapter 2, a century ago when Max Weber borrowed the term to describe a type of leader, he defined charisma as "the quality of an individual personality by which he is set apart . . . and treated as endowed with superhuman or exceptional powers." He called charisma an ideal type, something that is only approximated in reality. Weber also argued that charisma grows out of the relationship between the leader and his or her followers and is not just an individual trait of the leader. He said that personal charisma lasts only "as long as it receives recognition and is able to satisfy the followers or disciples."[4] In other words, there is a sociological as well as a psychological dimension to charisma. Unfortunately, this ambiguity about whether charisma inheres in the person or the relationship persists to this day and limits its usefulness as a scientific concept.

Does charisma originate in the individual, in the followers, or in the situation? Some theorists say all three.[5] According to psychoanalytic explanations, adult humans under certain circumstances are prone to regress to early stages of development and transfer to other people desires and fantasies from childhood. At the stage of primary narcissism, infants do not distinguish themselves from their mothers, and under conditions of personal or social crisis, troubled adults search for that lost paradise by making the leader the recipient of their desires for grandiosity.[6] Many of the cult leader Jim Jones's followers found that he provided an answer to their troubling personal needs. For Sigmund Freud, on the other hand, the appeal of charismatic leaders exists at a symbolic unconscious level where they represent the return of the primal father. The search for charismatic leaders grows out of people's need for order. Again, this need is likely to be more acute under crisis conditions—witness the Italy that produced Mussolini or the Germany that produced Hitler.[7] However, the exact combination of personality, followers, and situations that produces charisma has proven difficult to pin down. After surveying six theories of the origins of charisma, one study concludes that attempts to present an integrated model of charisma "have perhaps been premature."[8]

Another study looked at seven major political spellbinders of the twentieth century: Hitler, Mussolini, and Roosevelt in industrialized countries; Gandhi, Sukarno, Castro, and Khomeini in less developed countries. The author concluded that in all cases "charisma is found not so much in the personality of the leader as in the perceptions of the people he leads."[9] Ann Ruth Willner found that to locate the sources of charisma, she needed to look for the factors that called forth those perceptions and that they varied by culture and by time. She speculated that culture may explain why so few women charismatic leaders appear in political history; followers in most cultures have denied them the opportunity. Joan of Arc and Evita Peron are rare exceptions.

Social crises cause followers' distress, which leads them to turn to a leader and attribute charisma to him or her. But knowing that, leaders sometimes help to enlarge a crisis and exacerbate the distress that triggers the process of charisma creation. Compare two German crises and how leaders responded to them in the period between the world wars. Weimar Germany went through a crisis in 1923 when rampant inflation wiped out the savings of the middle class, but Gustav Stresemann, the dominant democratic leader at that time, chose to channel the discontent into an institutional parliamentary framework rather than a personal charismatic framework. A decade later, however, in the Depression of the 1930s, Adolf Hitler chose to exacerbate the crisis and undercut the parliament to focus followers' attention on his personal charisma as the solution. He then used the devices of the state to reinforce those impressions of charisma.

The attribution of charisma with which followers empower their leaders in such circumstances unleashes enormous amounts of energy on the part of both the leaders and the followers. It is unclear how long that extra energy can last. For Hitler, it began to decay as his success declined after 1943. For the assassinated Gandhi, it lasted past his death but gradually declined as a political force in independent India. The power that charismatic leaders unleash among their followers can do great good or great harm. Some theorists categorize "negative charismatics" as those who are prone to grandiose projects, inattention to details, unwillingness to delegate, failure to create institutions that empower followers, and lack of planning for their succession.[10] On the other hand, there have been historical moments when "positive" or "reparative" charismatic leaders like Gandhi, King, and Nelson Mandela have released energies among their followers that have transformed social and political situations for the better.

Charismatic leaders rely on personal and inspirational power resources more than the power that comes from holding an official position of authority such as monarch or president. Sometimes, however, the power attached to such offices can create an aura of charisma for their otherwise ordinary incumbents. Charismatic leaders are adept at communication, vision, confidence, being an exemplar, and managing the impressions they create. Some theorists distinguish between "close" charismatics, who work best in small groups or inner circles where the effects of their personality are felt directly, and "distant" charismatics, who rely on more remote theatrical performance to reach and move the broader imagined communities that they aspire to lead. In the first case, the personal charm is felt directly; in the latter case, it is projected and mediated. Other theorists distinguish "socialized" charismatics, who use their power to benefit others, and "personalized" charismatics, whose narcissistic personalities lead to self-serving behavior.[11]

Regardless of type, charisma is hard to identify in advance. A recent survey concluded that "relatively little" is known about what makes a leader charismatic. Some scholars treat charisma as well-developed social and political skills; others consider it an individual trait or attribute.[12] Dick Morris, an American consultant with a reputation for mastery of political manipulation, reports that in his experience, "charisma is the most elusive of political traits because it doesn't exist in reality; only in our perception once a candidate has made it by hard work and good issues."[13]

Similarly, the business press has described many CEOs as charismatic when things are going well, only to withdraw the label after they fail to make their numbers. For example, in May 2000 *Fortune* described John Chambers of Cisco as possibly the greatest CEO ever, but a year later, after a $400 billion decline in market value, it described him as naïve and believing too much in his own fairy tale.[14] Searching for corporate saviors has increasingly produced what Rakesh Khurana of Harvard Business School calls "the irrational quest for charismatic CEOs." He reports that companies often search for white knights with attractive images created by the media rather than those with the most appropriate managerial experience. Yet their charismatic image, however poorly it fits the company's internal needs, often helps to recruit resources such as capital and people from the outside world.[15] And resources help reinforce charisma. "In ancient times, leaders often wore special clothing, masks and ornaments that conferred on them a larger-than-life appearance"; for modern executives, "the same function is played by private planes, limousines, palatial homes, exclusive seats at sporting events, and other trappings of corporate power."[16]

Political scientists have tried to create charisma scales that would predict votes or presidential ratings, but these attempts have not proven fruitful. John F. Kennedy is often described as charismatic, but obviously not for everyone since he failed to capture a majority of the popular vote and his ratings oscillated during his presidency. Lyndon Johnson lamented that he lacked charisma; that was true of his relations with the broad public, but he could be quite magnetic and overwhelming in personal contacts. In a careful study of presidential rhetoric, the political scientist George Edwards found that even such famed orators as Franklin Roosevelt and Ronald Reagan could not count on charisma to generate support for their programs. Edwards concluded that charisma is more easily identified after the fact than before it—ex post rather than ex ante.[17] In that sense, the concept is too circular to have predictive power. Chinese emperors were once said to rule because they had "the mandate of heaven," and when they were overthrown it was because they had lost that special mandate. But no one could predict when that would happen. Similarly, success is often used to prove—after the fact—that a modern political leader has charisma, but it is hard to use charisma to predict who will be a successful leader.

Followers are more likely to attribute charisma to leaders when they feel a strong need for change, often in the context of a personal, organizational, or social crisis. As mentioned, the British public did not see Churchill as a charismatic leader in 1939, but a year later, his vision, confidence, and communications skills made him charismatic in the eyes of the British people given the anxieties they felt after the fall of France and the Dunkirk evacuation. Yet by 1945, when the public focus turned from winning the war to the construction of a welfare state, Churchill was voted out of office. His charisma did not predict his electoral defeat. The change in followers' needs was a better predictor.

In current usage, the word charisma has lost some of its mystery and simply become a vague synonym for "personal magnetism." We use it in the sense that people vary in their ability to attract others, and their attraction depends in part on inherent traits, in part on learned skills, and in part on social and political context. Some dimensions of attraction, such as appearances and nonverbal communication, can be tested. Various studies show that people who are rated as attractive are treated more favorably than unattractive people.[18] Looks also affect politics and elections; one study finds that a handsome man enjoys an edge over an ugly rival that is worth 6 to 8 percent of the vote. For women, the edge may be as much as 10 percent.[19] Psychologists have shown that the human face is a primary signal system for showing emotions.[20] Nonverbal signals account for a major part of human communications, and simple experiments have shown that some people communicate nonverbally better than others. For example, a Princeton study found that when people were shown images of two candidates in unfamiliar elections, they could predict the winners seven times out of ten.[21] A similar Harvard study that showed people ten-second silent video clips in fifty-eight elections found that their predictions explained 20 percent of the variation in the two-party vote—a more powerful variable than economic performance. Ironically, the predictions became poorer when the sound was turned on.[22] But these experiments test only part of what was traditionally described as charisma, and the overall concept remains problematic. Charisma is a usable concept only if we keep our eyes wide open and remember that it is an imprecise term for a personal magnetism that can vary with different followers and situations.

TRANSFORMATIONAL AND TRANSACTIONAL LEADERSHIP

Given the inadequate explanatory value of charisma alone, leadership theorists have incorporated it into a broader concept of transformational leadership. As one analyst put it, the new paradigm "tamed the original concept of charisma."[23] Transformational leaders empower and elevate their followers; they use conflict and crisis to raise their followers' consciousness and transform them. Transformational leaders mobilize power for change by appealing to their followers' higher ideals and moral values rather than their baser emotions of fear, greed, and hatred.

Transformational leaders induce followers to transcend their self-interest for the sake of the higher purposes of the group that provides the context of the relationship. Followers are thus inspired to undertake what Ronald Heifetz has termed "adaptive work" and do more than they originally expected based on self-interest alone. Charisma in the sense of personal magnetism is only one part of transformational leadership. As defined and operationalized by the leadership theorist Bernard Bass, transformational leadership also includes an element of "intellectual stimulation" (broadening followers' awareness of situations and new perspectives) and "individualized consideration" (providing support, coaching, and developmental experiences to followers rather than treating them as mere means to an end).[24] Thus a leader can be charismatic without being transformational, and vice versa. Transformational leaders who succeed may remain respected, but they may lose their aura of charisma as followers' needs change. Alternatively, charismatic leaders who come to believe they are truly exceptional may become autocratic and intolerant and no longer remain transformational.[25]

Transformational leaders are contrasted with transactional leaders, who motivate followers by appealing to their self-interest.[26] Transactional leaders use various approaches, but all rest on reward, punishment, and self-interest.[27] Transformational leaders appeal to the collective interests of a group or organization, and transactional leaders rely on the various individual interests. The former depend more on the soft power of inspiration, the latter on the hard power of threat and reward. Transactional leaders create concrete incentives to influence followers' efforts and set out rules that relate work to rewards.

The job of secretary-general of the United Nations involves very little hard power. As the quip goes, it is more secretary than general, and what hard power resources of money or forces the incumbent can muster have to be begged or borrowed from the member governments of the organization. A number of people have filled the post without great effect, but some have used their soft power resources for transformational purposes. For example, Dag Hammarskjöld seized the opportunity of the Suez Crisis created by Britain and France's invasion of Egypt in 1956 to persuade governments to create a new institution of UN peacekeeping forces, which is not mentioned in the original charter of the organization. In the wake of UN failures to prevent genocide and ethnic cleansing in Rwanda and Kosovo in the 1990s, Kofi Annan worked with others to persuade governments to recognize a new responsibility to protect endangered peoples.[28] Using primarily soft power to leverage the hard power of governments, these two leaders had transformational effects.

Just as hard and soft power can be complementary, the two types of leadership style are not mutually exclusive. Leaders can pick from a menu of hard and soft power resources. Many leaders use both styles at different times in different contexts. Achieving transformational objectives may require a combination of both hard and soft power, and the mix may change over time. In his early days at GE, the legendary CEO Jack Welch used a hard power top-down style to transform the company. "What got less press was how Welch subsequently settled into a more emotionally intelligent leadership style, especially when he articulated a new vision for the company and mobilized people to follow it."[29] Some hard power leaders have a vision that provides soft power. As mentioned earlier, Admiral Rickover, the creator of the American nuclear navy, used transactional hard power to threaten but combined it with a vision that attracted many excellent officers to work for him. As one study on leadership concluded, "Our results reveal that transformational and transactional leadership are so highly related that it makes it difficult to separate their unique effects."[30]

Although the term transactional is clear, the concept of transformation is confusing because theorists use it to refer to leaders' objectives, the styles they use, and the outcomes they produce.[31] Those three dimensions are not the same thing. Sometimes leaders transform the world but not their followers, or vice versa, and sometimes they use a transactional style to accomplish transformational objectives.

Consider the example of Lyndon Johnson. In the 1950s, Senator Johnson deeply wanted to transform racial injustice in the South, but he did not use soft power to preach to or inspire a new vision in other senators. Instead, he misled his fellow southerners about his intentions and used a transactional style of hard power bullying and bargaining to achieve progress toward his transformational objectives in passing a civil rights bill in 1957 that was anathema to many of the supporters who had made him majority leader.[32] He did not change his followers, but he did begin to change the world of African Americans in the South.

James MacGregor Burns, who in 1978 coined the term "transformational" to describe leadership, later added another word, "transforming," to refer to leaders' effects on their followers.[33] Franklin Roosevelt is often cited as an example of a transformational leader; in the 1930s, he used the soft power of inspirational communications to help achieve his transformational goals of social reform, transforming the views of his followers in the process. But after he failed to transform American isolationist attitudes, FDR used very indirect *transactional* bargaining to pursue his goal of moving U.S. foreign policy toward support of Great Britain before World War II. His followers were ready for transformation on social issues but not on foreign policy, and he was not able to transform the dominant public view until after the Japanese attack on Pearl Harbor in 1941. Harry Truman is another example of a successful leader who developed transformational objectives but tended to be transactional in his style.

Given this confusion in the theory, it is better to use different terms to describe leaders' objectives and their styles. With regard to leaders' objectives of changing the views of their followers, we can use Burns's term "transforming." In relation to changing the world, we can refer to leaders' objectives as ranging from status quo to transformational. We can distinguish leaders' styles by how they use hard and soft power resources. A leader may use both hard and soft power styles to achieve transformational objectives or incremental objectives or to preserve the status quo.

In democracies, force is not a significant option, so hard power resources of coercion and inducement consist mainly of hiring, firing, bullying, buying, and bargaining. The key soft power resources of inherent qualities and communications consist mainly of charismatic attraction, emotional inspiration, persuasion, and nonverbal communications. As Truman observed, "I sit here all day trying to persuade people to do the things they ought to have sense enough to do without my persuading them. . . . That's all the powers of the President amount to."[34] And CEOs struggling to merge newly acquired firms find that the hard power of firing people is rarely sufficient; it is equally important to create a soft power vision that attracts people to the merged corporate culture.

I use the terms "transactional style" to characterize what leaders do with their hard power resources and "inspirational style" to characterize leadership that rests more on soft power resources. Combining these two categories and using some well-known

TABLE 3.1 Leaders' Objectives and Styles

	Transactional Style	Inspirational Style
Transformational objectives	Lyndon Johnson	Franklin Roosevelt
Incremental objectives	Dwight Eisenhower	Bill Clinton

U.S. presidents as illustration produces the matrix in Table 3.1. It illustrates how one can have transformational leaders who mostly use a transactional style (Johnson), transformational leaders who are strong on inspirational style (Franklin Roosevelt), status quo leaders with a transactional style (Eisenhower), and incremental leaders who often use an inspirational style (Clinton).

Although this simple matrix helps to illustrate the point about differences in leaders' objectives and style, it would be more accurate to display leaders in various positions in a two-dimensional space rather than restrict them only to one of the four quadrants, since leaders adopt different styles in different contexts.[35] Moreover, change is a matter of degree. Not all leaders seek change, and many seek it on some issues and not others. Mu'ammar Qaddafi, the mercurial Libyan leader who has devoted his career to transformational objectives, told me that of the 190 people in the world who rule countries, most have no larger vision.[36] He is probably correct that most rulers and national leaders focus more on their personal power and perks than on dramatic change in their countries.

Sometimes leaders (and their followers) seek to preserve the status quo or adapt only slightly. As we will see, some business theorists define leadership in terms of change and contrast it with mere management. But this biases the concept against conservative leadership. Imagine an isolated monastery where monks want an abbot who does not introduce cable television or the Internet. Preserving a group's valued way of life can be an important form of leadership. Of course, in the dynamic world of modern business (where the identification of leadership with change originated), the status quo is often not an option, but that does not rule out conservative status quo leadership in all situations. By definition, transformational leaders seek major change, and their objectives can be scaled in terms of the degree and scope of change they seek.[37]

In any event, as I describe at length in the next chapter, the secret to success lies in the ability of leaders to combine hard and soft power resources in appropriate contexts. Michael Mumford and Judy Van Doorn describe such hybrid types as "pragmatic leaders." They use the example of Benjamin Franklin, who often wanted to change the status quo; Franklin did so not by inspirational appeal, but by careful analysis of social and power relations and then working (often behind the scenes) through elite networks to develop coalitions to implement his vision.[38] Table 3.2 illustrates how pragmatic leaders relate to close and distant followers.

Context determines how and when hard and soft power are used most effectively. One consideration is the coherence of the group in both its identity as a community and its cleavages over issues and problems. If a group is well integrated as a community

TABLE 3.2 Leaders' Style and Followers' Distance

	Mostly Transactional	Mixed (Pragmatic)	Mostly Inspirational
Inner circle	Nixon	Franklin	Truman
Distant public	Eisenhower	T. Roosevelt	Reagan

and has only minor differences over issues, limited objectives and a transactional style may suffice. Followers may be seeking conservative leadership that will protect a satisfactory status quo. If a group is well integrated in its identity but deeply divided over how to deal with its problems, a leader with a more inspirational, soft power style may be more effective. If a group is fragmented over both identity and issues, as is the case with many new nations, a combination of hard transactional and soft inspirational styles may be necessary for effectiveness.

Theorists argue that transactional leadership styles are more frequent and effective in stable and predictable environments, and an inspirational or soft power style is more likely in periods of rapid and discontinuous social and political change. Stable environments both allow and demand a broader range of styles to combine creativity with acceptance by important stakeholders. A company with a mature technology, stable growth, and a contented labor force will look for a style of leadership different from the style sought by a company facing turbulent markets, rapid technological change, and major outsourcing. Similarly, in political systems, a parliament, party, or bureaucracy will respond differently depending on context. Crisis conditions can liberate a gifted leader from the accumulated constraints of vested interest groups and bureaucratic inertia that normally inhibit action. Bill Clinton, caught up in the complacent 1990s, is said to have envied Franklin Roosevelt's crisis conditions of the 1930s. Potential followers experience new or accentuated needs; they look for new guidance; action becomes more fluid. George W. Bush used the crisis conditions after September 11, 2001, to make strong assertions of the executive power of the presidency as well as to invade Iraq (which many observers feel would not otherwise have obtained support). When followers feel the need for change, a leader with transformational objectives faces better odds, and an inspirational style is more likely to find responsive followers and to make their role more relevant.

CRITICAL SKILLS

What are the inspirational soft power skills and transactional hard power skills that leaders need to combine?[39] Three skills are particularly important for the soft power part of the mix: emotional intelligence, communications, and vision. The two key hard power skills are organizational and political. We will look at each in turn.

Emotional Intelligence

Emotional intelligence is the self-mastery, discipline, and empathic capacity that allows leaders to channel their personal passions and attract others.[40] Contrary to the view that emotions always interfere with thinking, emotional intelligence suggests that the ability to understand and regulate emotions can make overall thinking more effective.[41] It has two major components: mastery of the self and outreach to others. Although the name sounds modern, the idea is not new. In the 1920s, the psychologist E. L. Thorndike defined "social intelligence" as the ability to act wisely in human relations.[42] Practical people have always understood its importance in leadership. Supreme Court Justice Oliver Wendell Holmes famously quipped after meeting Franklin D. Roosevelt, "Second class intellect; first class temperament."[43] Most historians would agree that Roosevelt's success as a leader rested more on his emotional than his analytical IQ.

Psychologists have wrestled with measuring the concept of intelligence for more than a century. General IQ tests measure such dimensions of intelligence as verbal and spatial dexterity, but IQ scores can predict only about 10 to 20 percent of variations in success in academic achievement and occupational status. The 80 percent of success that remains unexplained is the product of hundreds of variables playing out over time. Emotional intelligence is one of them, but experts differ about how much of the variance it accounts for. Daniel Goleman, citing competency tests at 188 major companies, argues that emotional intelligence proves to be twice as important as technical or cognitive skills in terms of an employee's value to the company.[44] Others suggest it plays a more modest role.[45] Moreover, there is uncertainty about how the two aspects of emotional intelligence—self-control and empathy toward others—relate to each other. Clinton, for example, scores low on the first and very high on the second dimension. But there is general agreement that emotional intelligence is an important component of leadership, that it is a learnable skill that increases with age and experience, and that different people possess it in different degrees.

Emotional intelligence helps leaders manage their charisma or personal magnetism across changing contexts. Individuals present themselves to others in a variety of ways in order to manage the impressions they make.[46] Everyone has heard the expression "Dress for success"; politicians dress differently for different audiences. Reagan's staff was famous for its success in impression management. Even a tough general like George Patton used to practice his scowl in front of a mirror. Robert Mugabe, the autocratic president of Zimbabwe, is "a shrewd performer, switching from Shona to English to send different messages to different audiences."[47] If emotional intelligence is not authentic, others will likely find out in the long run, but successful management of personal impressions requires some of the same emotional discipline and skill possessed by good actors. Acting and leadership have a great deal in common. Reagan's prior experience served him well. Both he and Franklin Roosevelt were masters at projecting confidence and optimism. Despite FDR's pain and difficulty in moving on his polio-crippled legs, he maintained a smiling exterior and was careful to avoid being photographed in a wheelchair.

In business too, "managing for financial results . . . begins with the leader managing his inner life so that the right emotional and behavioral chain reaction occurs. . . . Moods that start at the top tend to move the fastest because everyone watches the boss."[48] Humans, like other primate groups, focus their attention on the leader. Closely watched CEOs and presidents are always conveying signals, whether or not they realize it. Emotional intelligence involves the awareness and control of such signals. It also involves self-discipline that prevents personal psychological needs from distorting policy. Richard Nixon, for example, was strong on vision and cognitive skills, but weak on emotional intelligence. He was able to strategize effectively on foreign policy but was less able to manage the personal insecurities that eventually led to his downfall.

George W. Bush showed emotional intelligence in mastering his problems with alcohol and in displaying courage to persevere in policies even when they were politically unpopular. But at some point, perseverance becomes emotional stubbornness that hinders learning and adjustment. In the view of the Canadian political leader Michael Ignatieff, "It was not merely that the president did not take the care to understand Iraq. He also did not take the care to understand himself. The sense of reality that might have saved him from catastrophe would have taken the form of some warning bell sounding inside, alerting him that he did not know what he was doing. . . . He had led a charmed life, and in charmed lives warning bells do not sound."[49] Like Woodrow Wilson before him, Bush's stubborn commitment to his vision inhibited learning.

Communications

An inspirational leader has to communicate effectively. Churchill often attributed his success to his mastery of English syntax. The ancient Greeks had schools of rhetoric to hone their skills for the assembly. Cicero made his mark in the Roman Senate after studying oratory. Good rhetorical skills help to generate soft power. Woodrow Wilson was not a gifted student as a child, but he succeeded in teaching himself oratory because he regarded it as essential for leadership. Martin Luther King Jr. benefited from growing up in an African American church tradition rich in the rhythms of the spoken word. Communication comes easier for some than others. Mario Cuomo, the former governor of New York (and no mean orator himself), compared Bill and Hillary Clinton: "She doesn't have the theatrical instinct that he has. She is more a Methodist and he is more theatrical."[50] Bill Clinton was able to combine a sense of theater with narrative stories and an overall ability to convey an argument. According to his staff, this was a skill he developed and improved gradually over his career.[51]

Oratory and inspirational rhetoric, however, are not the only forms of communication with which leaders frame issues and create meaning for their followers. Alan Greenspan, former chairman of the Federal Reserve Board, was far from an inspirational speaker, but markets and politicians hung on his every word and he carefully tailored the nuances of his language to reinforce the direction in which he wanted to lead monetary policy.[52] As we have seen, nonverbal signals are an important component of human communications; symbols and examples can be very effective. Some inspirational leaders such as Gandhi were not great orators, but the symbolism of his simple dress and lifestyle spoke louder than words. If one compares those images with pictures of the young, insecure Gandhi dressed as a proper British lawyer, one can see how carefully he understood symbolic communication. He ensured that actions such as the famous 1930 salt march to the sea had a slow pace that allowed the drama and tension to build. The march was designed for communication, not the ostensible reason of fabricating salt that the colonial government prohibited.

T. E. Lawrence ("of Arabia") also understood how to communicate with symbols. When he went to the Paris Peace Conference at the end of World War I, he flamboyantly wore Bedouin robes to dramatize the Arab cause. A year later, at a Cairo conference to negotiate boundaries in the region, he changed into a British officer's uniform to engage in the hard transactional bargaining.[53] To take a contemporary example, the British entrepreneur Richard Branson overcame dyslexia and poor academic performance to become a great success by using events and public stunts to promote his Virgin brands.[54]

In addition to communicating with distant audiences, leaders need the ability to communicate one-on-one or in small groups. In some cases, that close communication is more important than rhetoric. Organizational skills—the ability to attract and manage an effective inner circle of followers—can compensate for rhetorical deficiencies, just as effective public rhetoric can partly compensate for poor organizational skills. The inner circles of followers need to be attracted and inspired. Hitler was skillful at communicating with both distant and inner-circle audiences. Stalin relied primarily on the latter. Truman was a modest orator but compensated for his lack of public rhetoric by attracting and ably managing a stellar set of advisors. Leaders who lack great rhetorical skills can also communicate effectively by example, symbols, and actions. A good narrative is a great source of soft power, and the first rule that fiction writers learn about good narrative is to "show, not tell." Franklin Roosevelt used the

fictional story of lending a garden hose to a neighbor whose house
was on fire to explain to the American people his complex lend-
lease program before World War II. Reagan was a master of the
well-selected anecdote. Setting the right example is another crucial form of communication for leaders. Anticipating a skeptical
public reaction when Singapore raised the salaries of government
officials in 2007, Prime Minister Lee Hsien Loong announced that
he would forgo the raise for himself.

Vision

Part of what leaders communicate is vision, or skill in articulating
a picture that gives meaning to an idea and inspires others. It is
one of the ways that leaders help to create shared objectives.
Usually such visions provide a picture of the future and encourage
change, but some visions can portray the past or the status quo as
attractive and encourage people to resist change. Without a vision, it is difficult to lead others to change. Frederick Smith, CEO
of Federal Express, argues that "the primary task of leadership is to
communicate the vision and values of an organization."[55] When
Paul O'Neill became CEO of Alcoa, he chose workplace safety as
the core of his vision not only because it would be attractive to
workers, but "the better we got at that, the better we would get at
everything else."[56] On the other hand, some management experts
think it is more important to know your company well and pick
the right people than to worry about vision.[57]

   Some leaders think that vision can solve most of their problems,
but the wrong vision can do damage, and an overly ambitious
vision can also hurt. The two Bush presidents are often contrasted
in terms of vision. The elder Bush was faulted (and faulted himself)
for not having what he called "the vision thing." When pressed by
his staff to use more grandiose phrases in his speeches, he replied,

"It's just not me."[58] The younger Bush started with a vision of "compassionate conservatism" that initially served him well, but after the shock of the 9/11 attacks, he developed a far more ambitious vision of transforming the Middle East. The younger Bush had "an almost petulant heedlessness to the outside world" and was "irresistibly drawn to Big Ideas like bringing democracy to the Middle East, Big Ideas that stood in sharp contrast to the prudent small ball played by his father."[59] Yet the elder Bush turned out to have the better foreign policy. As the former German chancellor Helmut Schmidt once quipped, "People with vision should go see a doctor."[60]

Some aspiring leaders think that they must proclaim a vision that overawes their followers. In practice, however, a successful vision often arises from the needs of the group, which are then formulated and articulated by the leader. The vision that King expressed in his "I have a dream" speech was deeply rooted in the American dream and the African American experience. At the same time, the pressure to articulate a vision can get a leader into difficulty. As one university president put it, "Everyone asks, 'What's your vision?' But you offend many people and get into trouble by answering too quickly. The smart response at the beginning is 'What do you think?' and then listen before you articulate your vision."[61]

A successful vision has to be attractive to various circles of followers and stakeholders. What plays well with one group may not sit well with another. To be sustainable, a successful vision must also be an effective diagnosis of the situation a group faces. In choosing goals and articulating them in a vision, leaders need to analyze situations so that they get the question right before proposing answers. They need to not only solicit input from their followers but also to understand the context of their choices. They have to be able to accurately assess reality.

The boldness of a vision varies with the type of leadership involved. The leader of a social movement can call forth larger visions than those of a leader in a position of authority. At the time of the American Civil War, the social reformer William Lloyd Garrison could call for the immediate abolition of slavery, but Lincoln had to move more deliberately to preserve the union and avoid the secession of the border states that allowed slaveholding. A movement leader can promote a vision that is miles ahead of his followers, but a president with multiple objectives and responsibilities must maintain a continuous dialogue with the public that keeps him from moving too far ahead of his followers.[62] After former vice president Al Gore narrowly lost his bid for the presidency in 2000, he became a leader of the social movement to combat global climate change, his style changed from pragmatic to inspirational and prophetic, and he won a Nobel Peace Prize for his efforts.[63]

Analysts can judge the vision of a leader in authority in terms of whether it creates a sensible balance between realism and risk, and whether it balances objectives with capabilities. Anyone can produce a wish list, but effective visions combine inspiration with feasibility. To return to Tony Blair, one of his great strengths as a leader was his "ability to articulate a vision. A serious weakness has been his patchy attention to detail." As one of his cabinet members remarked, "You might have the Big Idea, you might have the energy to try to drive it through personally, but how did you actually make it work?"[64] Two twentieth-century American leaders, Woodrow Wilson and George W. Bush, were good at articulating an ambitious foreign policy vision but were poor at refining and reshaping their vision when they encountered challenges of implementation. Both promoted democracy, but both did so in a manner that generated a backlash against democracy promotion. Of course, prudence is not enough. Sometimes leaders need to stretch the boundaries of realism to inspire their followers and call forth extra effort, as Churchill did in 1940. But without a degree of prudence based on understanding of the context, visions turn from grand to grandiose and undercut the values they endeavor to promote. As Teddy Roosevelt once put it, "I hold the man worthless who is not a dreamer, who does not see visions; but I also hold him worthless unless in practical fashion he endeavors to shape his actions so that these dreams and visions can be partially realized."[65]

HARD POWER SKILLS

Two other skills are more closely related to transactional style and hard power.

Organizational Skills

Organizational skill is the ability to manage the structures, information flows, and reward systems of an institution or group. Leaders manage directly in regard to those who report to them, and they manage indirectly by establishing and maintaining systems for their institutions. This includes the encouragement of leadership at lower levels in their organizations. Especially important is the effective management of flows of information relating to both the inputs and outputs of decisions. Leaders must manage their inner circle of advisors to ensure an accurate flow of information and influence. They must avoid the emperor's trap of hearing only about the beauty of their new clothes. Ironically, George W. Bush, the first president with an MBA, was weaker on this dimension than his father, who, like Truman, knew how to manage an able group of advisors. For example, Stephen Hadley, who became the second Bush's national security advisor, is quoted as saying about Bush's first term, "I give us a B minus for policy development and a D minus for policy execution."[66]

Contemporary management theory has tended to distinguish the roles of leaders from those of managers and places greater emphasis on the former. In 1977, Abraham Zaleznik of Harvard Business School criticized management education and described managers as merely embracing process and seeking stability, while leaders tolerate risk and create change.[67] Organizations need both, but leaders are more scarce. As John Kotter, also of Harvard Business School, put it in describing corporate change, "A guiding coalition with good managers but poor leaders will not succeed."[68] Good leaders construct teams that combine these functions, making sure to hire subordinates who can compensate for the leader's deficiencies in managerial skills. More recently, there has been a renewed interest in leaders *as* managers. After all, vision without implementation is ineffective. Leaders need enough managerial skill to assure that systems are in place that provide the information needed for good decisions as well as effective implementation. An effective leader can take steps to manage and shape the context by creating and maintaining well-designed systems.

As James March of Stanford has written, well-designed systems are like stage directions in a play, and "organizations are stage managers."[69] They encourage actors to make correct entrances and exits without being told. But stage directions are not enough. People game systems for various reasons, and effective leaders play a critical role in maintaining the integrity of their systems. For example, if top leaders do not monitor their systems to ensure that they are producing full and accurate information flows, the systems are likely to become distorted by the most powerful subordinates. Under President George H. W. Bush, National Security Advisor Brent Scowcroft made sure that a set of powerful cabinet secretaries each had full access to the president. Under President George

W. Bush, many of the same strong personalities were involved, but the formal NSC system became distorted and produced a truncated flow of information. Secretary of State Colin Powell's chief of staff described the situation this way: "This furtive process was camouflaged neatly by the dysfunction and inefficiency of the formal decision-making process."[70] In the words of Army General Wayne Downing, who worked in the White House, "Over the years, the interagency system has become so lethargic and dysfunctional that it inhibits the ability to apply the vast power of the U.S. government on problems. You see this inability to synchronize in our operations in Iraq and in Afghanistan, across our foreign policy, and in our response to Katrina."[71] Similarly, in the private sector, one of Kenneth Lay's key leadership failures as CEO of Enron was in not permitting and responding in an appropriate way to bad news.

The organizational skills required for leaders *as* managers should not be confused with the efficiency or tidiness of a well-run organization. Nor should they be restricted to hierarchical bureaucratic organizations. Leaders of diffuse social movements also need to manage the inward and outward flows of information. In this broad sense, organization and management refer to leaders' ability to ensure an accurate inflow and outflow of information for making and implementing decisions. Effectiveness is more important than efficiency. Franklin Roosevelt, for instance, ran an inefficient organization with overlapping jurisdictions and responsibilities. It was costly in many ways, but it did assure him multiple competing flows of information. Richard Neustadt writes that Roosevelt "sought advice from everybody else that he could get his hands on: cabinet members, congressmen, and columnists, interest groups and partisans, citizens and friends. Roosevelt never thought that staffs had a monopoly on judgment or on information either."[72] Eisenhower ran an efficiently organized presidency that some at the time felt lacked leadership, but historians later discovered his hidden hand behind most important decisions.[73] Reagan practiced "extreme delegation," which worked when he had an able team in place but turned into a disaster when Donald Regan, John Poindexter, and Oliver North took over.[74] While Reagan excelled in the soft power skills of vision, communication, and emotional intelligence, he lacked the transactional skills of leadership as management. Successful business leaders combine these skills. As the management expert Tom Peters has argued, top business managers cannot hope to solve all problems in a tidy fashion, but "what they can do is: (1) generally shape business values, and (2) educate by example."[75] A crucial component for such an example is assuring that unfiltered bad news can reach the leaders and be acted on promptly.

Machiavellian Political Skills

Political skills are crucial for effective leadership, but they are more complex than first appears. Politics can take a variety of forms. Intimidation, manipulation, and negotiation are related to hard power, but politics also includes inspiration, brokerage of new beneficial arrangements, and developing networks of trust typical of soft power. Politics can involve not just success in achieving goals for oneself and a narrow group of followers, but also building political capital for bargaining with wider circles of followers. When Roderick Kramer calls "political intelligence" the ability to size up the weaknesses, insecurities, likes, and dislikes of others so that you can turn them into your instruments, he is referring narrowly to the Machiavellian political skills that are crucial for the hard power of threats and inducements.

Kramer's "great intimidators" employ a variety of tactics to bully and intimidate others in order to get what they want. Abusive language or an aloof attitude can throw others off-balance, and a calculated loss of temper can be useful at times. Former secretary of defense Robert McNamara shared intimacies with superiors but never with subordinates. Both he and Margaret Thatcher intimidated others by appearing to know it all—even when they did not. Kramer describes former CEO Carly Fiorina of Hewlett Packard and Disney's Michael Eisner as skillful "silent intimidators."[76] Lyndon Johnson, on the other hand, would physically get up front and personal, draping an arm around shorter men and seizing others by their lapels to argue while pressing his face close to theirs.[77] He would also offer visitors a seat in a low, soft chair while he loomed over them in a tall rocking chair with a high seat. Robert Mugabe uses the silent treatment, "refusing, for example, to say a word in one-on-one meetings, to the deep consternation of the other party."[78]

Kramer contrasts such hard "political intelligence" with the "social intelligence" emphasized by current leadership theorists that stresses empathy and interpersonal, soft power skills that attract followers and extract maximum performance from subordinates. Socially aware executives are also experts at reading the currents of office politics and using political skills in the broader sense of the term, but the starkest point of contrast between these two kinds of leaders is how willing they are to use hard power skills.

The psychologist David McClelland has shown that people with a strong need for power are more effective leaders, but only if they also develop an internal capacity to restrain their use of power.[79] Kramer points out that his great intimidators are "bullies with a vision," aiming at an objective rather than just manipulating others to prove who is the stronger. Pure bullying—defined as repeated actions designed to humiliate and dominate others—tends to be counterproductive, though it is a common human behavior.

Researchers have concluded that 7 to 15 percent of the school-age population can be characterized as bullies.[80] In the American workplace, 37 percent say they have been bullied, and of those, nearly half say they left their job as a result.[81] As a form of power behavior, bullying can be self-gratifying and tactical or carefully strategic. It can be successful or unsuccessful. The legendary basketball coach Bobby Knight was both a bully and effective.[82] Studies of the workplace, however, have shown that pervasive bullying often lowers performance, and notable bullies like Al Dunlap of Scott Paper created a culture that destroyed the company.[83] In politics, efforts to rate leaders on a scale of Machiavellianism have had mixed results. One study finds Machiavellianism negatively correlated to leaders' performance, but a study of charismatic U.S. presidents finds a positive relationship between Machiavellianism and performance.[84]

Daniel Goleman and his colleagues report that in "some specific business cases, an SOB boss resonates just fine. But in general, leaders who are jerks must reform or else their moods and actions will eventually catch up with them."[85] The politics of fear can be effective, but they are not the only political skills, nor the best skills in all circumstances. On the contrary, some leaders build and empower teams. The soft power politics of attraction may be even more effective when they call forth additional effort and loyalty and thus add leverage to the leader's power. Lincoln included his rivals for the presidency in his cabinet and then used primarily soft political skills to coax significant contributions from them.[86] Too much hard Machiavellian power can interfere with and deprive leaders of their soft power.

Moreover, a style that works in one context may not work in another. Kramer describes former secretary of the treasury and Harvard president Larry Summers as trying to shake up Harvard with a pattern of initial confrontation, followed by skeptical

TABLE 3.3 Effective Leadership Styles: Soft and Hard Power Skills

Soft Power (Inspirational)

1. Emotional IQ	—Ability to manage relationships and charisma
	—Emotional self-awareness and control
2. Communications	—Persuasive words, symbols, example
	—Persuasive to near and distant followers
3. Vision	—Attractive to followers
	—Effective (balance ideals and capabilities)

Hard Power (Transactional)

1. Organizational capacity	—Manage reward and information systems
	—Manage inner and outer circles (direct and indirect leadership)
2. Machiavellian skills	—Ability to bully, buy, and bargain
	—Ability to build and maintain winning coalitions

Smart Power (Combined Resources)

1. Contextual IQ (broad political skills)	—Understand evolving environment
	—Capitalize on trends ("create luck")
	—Adjust style to context and followers' needs

and hard questioning to get people to think more deeply about their purpose in the institution.[87] But the case is also illuminating for another reason. Although Summers had been successful in Washington and wisely proposed a sound vision for the university, he was less successful in executing that vision and resigned prematurely. Professor Jay Lorsch of the Harvard Business School summarized the situation of Harvard presidents: "This person who could be a powerful president really finds himself checked not only by the people above him but by the deans and the faculties around him."[88] In this context of constrained power resources, in contrast to Washington, Summers failed to combine hard and soft power successfully. In a decentralized university like Harvard (and many other nonprofit institutions), presidents have much more limited hard power resources than do their equivalents in government and business. In such a context, once their hard power tactics undercut their soft power, they have few power resources left.

The moral of the story, of course, is not that hard or soft power is better, or that an inspirational or a transactional style is the answer, but that it is important to understand how to combine these power resources and leadership styles in different contexts. Table 3.3 summarizes these soft and hard power skills and introduces a sixth critical skill: the ability to understand context so that hard and soft power can be successfully combined into a smart power strategy.[89] A strategy is a plan that relates ends and means, goals and tactics, and such plans must vary according to context.[90] Strategic resourcefulness can sometimes compensate for lack of resources and explain why David can defeat Goliath or some organizations and social movements succeed where better endowed ones fail. An effective leader must have contextual intelligence in order to develop smart strategies. We turn to that skill in the next chapter.

FOUR

Contextual Intelligence

Leadership is a power relationship between leaders and followers, but as we saw earlier, power depends on context. That brings us to the third main point in the conceptual triad of leaders: followers and context.

General Electric prides itself on producing leaders, but as we have seen, half of GE highfliers who went on to become CEOs of other Fortune 500 companies had disappointing records. A major reason for their success or failure was whether their new companies needed the skills they had honed at GE or whether they faced a context requiring a different set of skills. When Intuit CEO Steve Bennett was asked what would have happened if he had taken Jack Welch's tough approach at GE and applied it at a Silicon Valley software company like Intuit, he replied, "I would have gotten voted off the island. Ultimately, that is the consequence of taking these rote things that you learn at GE or any other company and misapplying them."[1] Ironically, shortly thereafter, Bennett, who was known as a tough manager, lost his job as CEO when Intuit profits suffered a downturn.

James Webb, who ably ran the Bureau of the Budget for Harry Truman, proved less successful when the president moved him into the number two slot in the State Department, but he later went on to great success as director of NASA. Webb's quantitative skills and efforts to measure performance worked well in two of the jobs, but were inappropriate for diplomacy. As Richard Neustadt concluded, "From one situation to the next, the... leader's influence swells or diminishes depending on how personal operating style fits organizational needs and outside conditions."[2] Lyndon Johnson was one of the greatest majority leaders in the history of the Senate, but not one of the greatest foreign policy presidents. George W. Bush was often described as a successful managing partner of the Texas Rangers baseball team and a consensual governor of Texas; his performance in Washington proved more controversial.

Why do some leaders succeed in one context and fail in another? A common answer is "Horses for courses": some horses run better on a dry track and some on a muddy course. Leaders' skills fit some situations better than others—witness the cases of Churchill and Giuliani discussed earlier. Lech Walesa, the heroic Polish shipyard worker whose physical courage in resisting a repressive Communist government attracted followers to join the Solidarity movement, found himself uncomfortable and unsuccessful when he subsequently was in the post-Communist government.[3] Many a good CEO turns out to be a disappointment when appointed as a cabinet secretary. A street gang leader lacks skills to be a successful academic, and vice versa. As one theorist summarized, leadership is "an interactive art" in which the leader is "dancing" with the context, the problem, the factions, and the objective.[4]

Some leaders tend to be relationship-oriented; their self-esteem as a leader comes more from developing good personal relationships with their followers. Other leaders are more task-oriented; their satisfaction comes from the accomplishment of a task. The former tend to rely more on inspirational skills and soft power, the latter more on transactional skills and hard power. But success in both cases depends on their understanding their own motives and adapting their skills to the degree of control they experience in different situations. The nature of the group, the clarity of the task, and the resources of their position all determine situational control.[5]

At one stage in the 1960s, theorists developed a "contingency" theory of leadership and hoped for a "science of situations" that would allow accurate predictions. But such aspirations fell victim to the overabundance of variables that plague leadership studies. As one critic put it, "What counts as a situation and appropriate response is interpretive and contestable."[6] In studying the success and failure of team leaders, the psychologists Richard Hackman and Ruth Wageman concluded that there is no one way to lead a team. Success depends on the accuracy and completeness of the leader's mental model of the situation, skill in executing the behaviors required by that model, and the ability to harvest the lessons of experience.[7] Although there is no predictive science of situations, there are important differences that leaders can intuit.

Anthony Mayo and Nitin Nohria of Harvard Business School have defined contextual intelligence as the ability to understand an evolving environment and to capitalize on trends.[8] They use the concept to explain why some firms they studied responded more successfully than others to changing markets over the past century. More specifically, contextual intelligence is an intuitive diagnostic skill that helps a leader to align tactics with objectives to create smart strategies in varying situations. Others have called it judgment or wisdom, an "acquaintance with relevant facts of such a kind that it enables those who have it to tell what fits with what; what can be done in given circumstances and what cannot, what means will work in what situations and how far, without necessarily being able to explain how they know this or even what they know."[9]

Contextual intelligence implies both a capability to discern trends in the face of complexity and adaptability while trying to shape events. Bismarck once referred to this skill as the ability to intuit God's movements in history and seize the hem of his garment as he sweeps by.[10] As an American political scientist describes the process of government, leaders and policy entrepreneurs "do more than push, push, push for their proposals or for their conception of problems. They also lie in wait—for a window to open." Like surfers, "their readiness combined with their sense for riding the wave and using the forces beyond their control contributes to success."[11] In unstructured situations, it is often more difficult to ask the right questions than to get the right answer. Leaders with contextual intelligence are skilled at providing meaning or a road map by defining the problem that a group confronts. They understand the tension between the different values involved in an issue and how to balance what is desirable with what is feasible.

Contextual intelligence requires using the flow of events to implement a strategy. It allows leaders to adjust their style to the situation and to their followers' needs. It enables them to create flows of information that educate their hunches. It involves the broad political skill of not only sizing up group politics, but of understanding the positions and strengths of various stakeholders so as to decide when and how to use transactional and inspirational skills. It is the self-made part of luck. One of the reasons for Churchill's skill at contextual intelligence was his immersion in history through writing a two-volume biography of his politician father, a five-volume history of World War I, and a four-volume study of his ancestor the Duke of Marlborough.[12]

Psychologists generally agree that multiple forms of intelligence exist. What we today measure as IQ was originally developed a century ago in the context of the French school system, and thus it focuses on linguistic, mathematical, and spatial skills that tend to predict success in school (though not necessarily in life). Many psychologists define intelligence as the ability to solve problems or create products that are valued in one or more cultural settings.[13] This involves a collection of intelligences, but some psychologists are concerned that if we use the word too broadly to refer to any skills or dispositions, it loses usefulness. Some argue, for example, that for a skill to be an intelligence, it should have some overlapping correlation with general intelligence.[14] The idea of contextual intelligence meets that requirement. It consists partly of cognitive analytic capabilities and partly of tacit knowledge built up from experience. Tacit knowledge tends to be implicit and inarticulate, or expressed in rules of thumb. In some situations, such street smarts are much more important to success than school smarts. For example, tests have shown that the most effective fire chiefs in an emergency are not those with the highest measured IQ scores, but those with tacit knowledge of context built from experience.[15]

Contextual intelligence is also correlated with the skill of emotional intelligence discussed in chapter 3. Without sensitivity to the needs of others, pure cognitive analysis and long experience may prove insufficient for effective leadership. Those who object to applying the word intelligence to this set of skills can think of the skill as "contextual acuity" or contextual "judgment."[16] The important point is not the word but the skill.[17] Reagan, for example, was often faulted on his pure cognitive skills, but he generally had good contextual intelligence. Jimmy Carter had good cognitive skills, but was often faulted on his contextual intelligence. As one wag put it, he was better at counting the trees than seeing the forest.

George W. Bush has famously described his leadership role as being "the decider." But deciding how and when to decide is as important as making the final decision.[18] What should be the composition of the group the leader turns to? What is the context of the decision? How will information be communicated, and how much control does the leader maintain over the decision? A leader who gets any of these factors wrong may be decisive, but also decisively wrong. Bush described his leadership as having three core components: outline a vision, build a strong team, and delegate much of the process to them.[19] His decision making on Iraq, however, has been criticized for the grandiosity of his vision, his failure to manage the divisions in his team, and his failure to monitor the delegation of decisions. Without contextual intelligence, being a "decider" is not enough.

Understanding context is crucial for effective leadership. Some situations call for autocratic decisions, and some require consensus. Ronald Heifetz argues that the first thing a leader needs to diagnose is whether the situation calls for technical and routine solutions or requires adaptive change. In the former case, the leader may want to clarify roles and norms, restore order, and quickly provide a solution. In the latter case, the leader may want to let conflict emerge, challenge unproductive norms and roles, and let the group feel external pressures in a range it can stand so that it learns to identify and master the adaptive challenge. This may require delaying a decision. Leaders are often tempted to decide quickly to reduce followers' anxieties rather than to use the anxieties as a learning experience. As Hackman and Wageman put it, "The impulse to get things taken care of sooner rather than later (for example, when conflicts about how best to proceed with the work become intense) can be almost irresistible. It takes a good measure of emotional maturity to resist such impulses."[20] In Heifetz's useful metaphors, a leader needs to gain perspective by "going to the balcony" to observe the swirling activity on the dance floor, regulate the "level of distress," "give the work back to the people," and protect "voices from below." This is a very different image of the work of leadership than simply to be "the decider."[21]

Interesting cases occur when leaders are able to transfer their skills across contexts. Eisenhower, for example, was successful both as a military leader and as a president. Many leaders have a fixed repertoire of skills, which limits and conditions their responses to new situations. Quantitative measurement was the sharpest arrow in James Webb's quiver, but it failed to penetrate the diplomatic culture of the State Department. Other leaders have a wider repertoire and a better idea of which arrows to select under which circumstances; to use an information age metaphor, they have a broader bandwidth and are able to tune carefully for different situations.[22] That set of skills is contextual intelligence.

There is a wide variety of contexts in which leaders have to operate, but the following five dimensions are particularly important for the intuitive skill of contextual intelligence: culture, distribution of power resources, followers' needs and demands, time urgency, and information flows.

UNDERSTANDING CULTURAL CONTEXT

Culture is the recurrent pattern of behavior by which groups transmit knowledge and values. Almost all human groups develop cultures, and they exist at multiple levels. Some aspects of human culture are universal; other dimensions are particular to a group.

The culture of the group sets the framework for leaders: "Culture and leadership are two sides of the same coin in that leaders first create cultures when they create groups and organizations. Once cultures exist, they determine the criteria for leadership and thus determine who will or will not be a leader." Managing culture is one of the most important things that leaders do. If leaders do not "become conscious of the cultures in which they are embedded, those cultures will manage them."[23]

The psychological needs of followers to attribute charisma to leaders in times of personal or social need may be true of many groups, but the particular traits vary across cultures: "A charismatic leader of one organization does not necessarily capture the hearts and minds of followers from a different type of organization." Although Gandhi influenced King, Gandhi's style was very Indian and King's very American. To take a business example, a new American boss in a Mexican plant fraternized with subordinates to create a friendly climate in the workplace, but his Mexican managers (who relied on cultural values of hierarchy and authority) rebelled because their power base was undermined.[24] Effective leaders inspire followers through the careful management of emotion, but appropriate levels of emotional expression vary with cultures. Japan is not Italy. A Thai sees more than twenty separate smiles providing subtle cues where a Canadian sees only one "friendly smile."[25]

Cultural intelligence is as important to leadership of social movements as it is to leadership of organizations. In the 1990s, two new movements burst on the Mexican political scene devoted to improving the condition of the rural Indian population. The Zapatista Army of National Liberation was relatively successful, while the Popular Revolutionary Army (EPR) failed in parallel efforts to mobilize a mass base and foreign support. Though Subcomandante Marcos, the leader of the former, was a non-Indian former university professor, he spent a decade in the jungle and altered the group's ideology and strategies to fit the cultural worldview of the local Indian population. At the same time, his urban middle-class background allowed him to reshape the movement's rhetoric and tactics to appeal to the interests and culture of distant audiences. In contrast, the leaders of the EPR were unable to adjust their Marxist ideology to fit either the local culture or the new political culture in distant media capitals in a post–cold war era.[26]

Microcultures such as a club or a workplace require as much cultural intelligence as do national cultures. Many a corporate merger that looked lucrative to investment bankers because of economic synergies and opportunities comes a cropper because of cultural differences. For example, cultural differences led many senior people to leave Chrysler after it merged with Daimler-Benz in 1998. In contrast, IBM has a special team of employees who work full time on postdeal cultural issues, and six months after a deal closes, the leaders of the acquired company, along with leaders from other acquired companies, discuss their own perspectives on IBM's management, leadership, products, and services. According to IBM's global director of human resources, "One of the dangers in any acquisition is the acquiring company assuming their culture is the right one. . . . If you tell me how to make me better, you open up a dialogue. We build a bond and we build a culture."[27] When the defense contractor Raytheon acquired a rival firm, the cultures were similar, but the CEO realized, "We had been their enemy for years and they hated our guts." Rather than try to indoctrinate his new employees into an existing Raytheon culture, he articulated a new vision of perfection in production as the goal for the merged company and adjusted rhetoric and rewards to reinforce this new culture.[28] The 9/11 Commission attributed the failure to "connect the dots" of intelligence in advance of the

September 11 attacks in part to cultural differences that inhibited communications between the FBI and the CIA. The FBI law enforcement culture sought and communicated information in relation to preparing cases for trial and convictions, while the CIA intelligence culture treated information as a continuing flow to be protected for future monitoring and warning.[29]

Culture is not static, but it tends to change slowly. People get set in their habits, particularly when values are involved. But sometimes events and policies can speed up change. Take offshore oil platforms, which are known for a macho culture of men working in isolation from the rest of society. When an oil company discovered that a high rate of accidents was cutting profitability, it introduced sensitivity training, rewarded cooperation, and changed the culture from a macho stereotype in the direction of a more caring and cooperative culture, and the rate of accidents declined.[30] Leaders with contextual intelligence understand that policy change sometimes requires a change of group culture, and they develop a sense of how malleable a given culture can be under different circumstances.

Even at the national level, impressive cultural changes can occur. Japan had a militaristic culture in the 1930s, but changed to "Japan Inc.," with an intense economic focus, after the shock of losing World War II. A Japanese leader cannot come to power today with the bellicose and nationalistic style that would have been essential in the 1930s. Economic and social trends also produce cultural change. A century ago, China's poor economic performance was attributed to its Confucian culture, and India was said to be limited to a "Hindu rate of growth." Today both are ranked among the fastest growing economies in the world, and Chinese and Indian political leaders now depend heavily on economic growth for their legitimacy.

Asian companies are known for having a secretive, family style of leadership, but this culture may be changing. Quinn Mills of Harvard Business School speculates, "As Asian companies rely more on professional employees of all sorts, and as professional services become more important in Asian economies, the less autocratic and more participative and even empowered style of leadership will emerge. Asian leadership will come to more resemble that of the West."[31] At the same time, it is unlikely that all aspects of cultures will converge under the pressures of modernization and globalization. Japan has weathered a century and a half of responses to globalization, but no one would say that its culture resembles that of Europe or the United States.

A Dutch scholar observes that "leadership in Holland presupposes modesty, as opposed to assertiveness in the United States. No U.S. leadership theory has room for that." In his view, American culture skews American management theories, which feature three elements not present in other countries: market processes, emphasis on the individual, and a focus on managers rather than workers.[32] But a single European culture does not exist. Theorists have identified at least four patterns in Europe: Anglo market orientation, French pyramidal structures, Scandinavian consensual approach, and German machine efficiency. A European leader has to understand these differences. A two-hour meeting in Germany may take all day in southern Italy.[33] Even though all three are primarily German-speaking countries, Germany, Austria, and Switzerland have significant cultural differences.[34]

At the national level, a comprehensive review of nearly four hundred studies concluded that a country's cultural values will determine the optimum leadership profile for that country.[35] The GLOBE Project administered 17,300 questionnaires in sixty-two societies, and on that basis identified ten cultural clusters with different leadership characteristics: Latin America, Anglo, Latin Europe, Nordic Europe, Germanic Europe, Eastern Europe, Confucian Asia, Southern Asia, Sub-Saharan Africa, and the Middle East.[36] And within each of these clusters, national, regional, local, religious, organizational, and other subcultures exist. Leaders face daunting challenges in understanding national differences in cultural context.

When encountering different environments, whether national or organizational, some people are better than others at learning the appropriate cues to figure out quickly what is happening in a culture. Such skills can also be learned. Just as some people are naturals in learning foreign languages while others have to struggle, similar patterns exist in cultural intelligence (which is a subset of contextual intelligence). People can alert themselves or be trained to increase the complexity of their thinking, experience cross-cultural settings, overcome negative stereotypes, and imagine other cultural viewpoints.[37] This also requires that leaders become aware of the way their communications affect multiple audiences. For example, Bush's rhetoric about a war between good and evil proved effective in rallying American followers after September 11, 2001, but proved counterproductive in attracting allies in Europe and the Muslim world. Effective leadership in a globalizing world will require leaders to learn this kind of contextual intelligence.

DISTRIBUTION OF POWER RESOURCES

A second crucial dimension of contextual intelligence is the ability to intuit and assess the distribution of power resources in a group. Leaders must not only understand the political culture of a group, but they must also assess how it relates to networks and the distribution of hard and soft power resources that will be available and the costs of their use. Culture and power are closely related, since which resources produce power in a given domain depends heavily on the objectives that are expressed in a culture. An army general faces a different set of options from those that confront a church pastor. The culture of a government is different from the culture of a nonprofit organization, just as the culture of a marine platoon is different from the culture of a social club. Even in similar domains, behavior that is appropriate in a software company differs from what is acceptable in an open source community.

A group's political culture as well as its formal structures and unwritten rules determine what power resources are available to leaders in any particular situation, which in turn shapes their choice of transactional and inspirational styles. Institutional structures and group cultures authorize and discourage certain actions. As we saw earlier, successful hunters in some hunter-gatherer tribes need to be extremely modest about their skills and kills lest others in the group decide to cut them down to size. Leading others who consider themselves the leaders' equals is different from commanding troops where hierarchy is the norm. Running a law firm or consulting partnership is different from running a manufacturing corporation. Many of these people do not consider themselves followers but independent elites. They respond poorly to a command-and-control style and have the power to resist their formal leaders.[38]

Even when the political culture is not overly egalitarian, leaders need to understand whether they are in an executive or a legislative situation. In the latter case, the only hope of success is to assemble majority coalitions. A CEO like Ross Perot had less need to assemble coalitions inside his company than Lyndon Johnson did in the Senate. In the White House, Johnson needed different political skills (for example, public rhetoric to express a vision and managerial skills to implement it) from those he needed in the

Senate. Closely related to the legislative structure is the ability to assess what constitutes a minimum winning coalition. It is often impossible or too costly for a leader to win everyone to a common position, but some followers bring more companions into the fold than others. Understanding the shapes of such possible winning (or blocking) coalitions is essential in coping with flat power structures where there is very little hierarchical authority.

Leaders also need to understand the sources of their authority. Power may be distributed broadly or narrowly throughout a group or organization, and leaders can act with or without authority, but they must understand the authoritative context.[39] Sometimes official status conveys a good deal of authority and sometimes it does not. Leaders can generate informal authority, as when Rosa Parks refused to give up her bus seat in Montgomery or young students conducted sit-ins at segregated lunch counters during the civil rights movement of the 1960s. In other power structures, such as the British monarchy, formal authority has strictly limited power. A university president who tries to shape her professors' research will quickly exceed the bounds of her authority.

Leaders also have to be able to assess the strength of loyalties that exist in small groups and in wider imagined communities. Where identities are strong and noble purposes predominant, an inspirational call to serve the group can generate considerable soft power. In other circumstances, such efforts may merely produce cynicism and a backlash of negative reactions; an appeal to tangible interests and rewards would be more effective. For example, in bargaining over wages, inspirational appeals and symbols of soft power are more likely to be successful in a nonprofit situation than in a corporate setting where workers believe the employer has deep pockets.

Another aspect of power assessment is the need to understand the symmetrical or asymmetrical nature of the interdependence leaders share with other members of the group. To paraphrase the economist Albert Hirschman: What options do others have for exit, voice, or loyalty, and how does that affect their power?[40] As described earlier, leaders must understand the structure of the networks in which they are involved and the value of strong and weak ties in different situations. They must also know the structure of incentives in the game that is being played. Is it positive or zero sum? If it resembles a zero-sum prisoners' dilemma in which one's loss is the other's gain, will it go on long enough that the other can be taught an optimal cooperative strategy of tit for tat, or will the game end too soon for such a strategy to succeed?[41] Some of these skills in political assessment can be taught; some come naturally (or not at all). But they all are critical to contextual intelligence.

Finally, in modern democratic societies, leaders need to understand the difference between the politics of public and the politics of private contexts and how that affects the distribution of power. The cultural difference between the public and private sectors has a strong effect on the power resources and styles that leaders find effective. Public groups usually involve a wider and more diverse set of stakeholders who can claim a legitimate voice. Measures of merit, such as profit, are more precise and less contested in private organizations. Efficiency often takes second place to considerations of due process in making public decisions, and secrecy and confidentiality are more restricted. The very publicness of public groups and organizations—sometimes described as making decisions in a fishbowl—constrains certain power resources and affects choices of style. Very often, successful business leaders who go into government fail because of inattention to these cultural differences and the ways they affect the distribution of power resources.[42] When people say these businesspeople "lack political skills," they are referring to knowledge of the political culture of the public sector and how it affects power resources. In the private world of the corporate hierarchy in which they previously succeeded, such leaders almost certainly used impressive but more narrowly defined political skills.

FOLLOWERS' NEEDS AND DEMANDS

Another aspect of contextual intelligence is the ability to grasp the changing needs and demands of potential followers. How stable is the status quo? How much do people feel a need for change, and what types of change do they want? Leaders must diagnose what it will take to get followers to engage in painful change.[43] They must ask where resistance to change will be located, and what actions and messages can persuade people to do painful but adaptive work. How can coalitions be created to overcome resistance? How can hard power be used to overcome resistance without undercutting the power of attraction and co-optation?

Leaders also need to assess contexts in terms of their followers' demand to participate in decisions. The Yale professor Victor Vroom distinguishes "autocratic situations," which invite hard power approaches, from "autocratic managers," who always use such a style. His research shows that the situational context is considerably more important than the managers' traits. In his words, "Leaders must have the capabilities of being both participative and autocratic and of knowing when to employ each."[44]

Vroom distinguishes degrees of autocracy on a five-point scale: (1) making decisions alone, (2) deciding after individual consultation, (3) deciding in the context of group consultation, (4) facilitating decisions by others, and (5) delegating fully to others. In some situations, others do not want to be consulted but simply want someone to make quick and effective decisions. In other situations, a leader's failure to consult others can create great discontent and even rebellion. For example, in my own experience as an academic administrator, I had to learn which decisions (sometimes important ones over budget and fund-raising) the faculty did not want me to bother them with, and on which ones they insisted on having key input (faculty appointments).

Among the key determinants of a leader's choice of appropriate style in a given context is the amount of expertise a decision requires, the timeliness of a decision, the cost of waiting for broader consultation, and the type of change that is needed. But even when followers are willing to allow autocratic decision making, a leader may opt for broader participation in order to educate followers and to develop a sense of commitment and ownership of the decision. As we saw earlier, when a leader thinks that a group is facing a situation that requires adaptive change, he or she may refuse to make a quick decision that relieves tensions and instead insist on giving the work back to the people as a way to educate them about change.

The novelty of a situation also affects leaders' choices of style. In familiar situations, the problem may be primarily one of co-ordination and action. An effective leader must determine what types of decision-making procedure would work best in a particular context. In a routine situation, it may be sufficient to consult a limited set of participants. But in a novel situation, effective leadership may require greater diversity in the group that shapes decisions. Although broader participation could slow things down, it also assures a broader set of views and the avoidance of groupthink. The increased transactions costs may be more than rewarded by the greater creativity of a more diverse group. In the failed Bay of Pigs invasion of 1961, John F. Kennedy followed standard bureaucratic procedures and received a predictable framework of advice. He learned from this lesson, however, and in his successful handling of the Cuban Missile Crisis in 1962, he created a more diverse group and set of procedures to inform his decisions.[45]

CRISIS AND TIME URGENCY

A crisis is a turning point in an unstable situation, and it generally implies urgency in terms of time. But sometimes urgency merely means an importunate or pressing problem that persists over long periods, and people use the term "crisis" as a metaphor for long-drawn-out processes that challenge important values. Historians refer to the crisis of the French monarchy in the decades that preceded the French Revolution. Business journalists refer to the crisis of the American car companies as their market share declines. Ecologists refer to the crisis of global warming and the catastrophic consequences that may occur by the end of the century. In this metaphorical sense, when crises emerge slowly, leaders have more options and time to develop strategies. Leaders often welcome a sense of crisis because it relaxes the normal constraints that limit their power and actions. In the context of long-drawn-out threats to group values, leaders may even try to create a sense of urgency. Conflicts within a group can help build a sense of urgency, and leaders have to manage conflicts without settling issues too quickly. People need time to learn and adapt. Heifetz uses the metaphor of a pressure cooker and a leader's ability to understand the strength of the institutions that he or she uses to contain the pressure.[46] Creating a sense of crisis is one of the tools that leaders use to educate followers about the need for adaptive change. Crises provide teaching moments and open windows of opportunity for change.

Crisis can also be defined more specifically as a situation in which there is a threat to key values and a premium on timely response. Time-sensitive crises create a very different context from slowly developing or emergent crises. Leaders' options are more limited by time, but the visible dramatization of urgency increases others' willingness to grant leaders exceptional powers. Such contexts require a different set of skills, including mental preparation, calm under stress, and the ability to communicate to and reassure followers. These were the skills that Giuliani demonstrated on September 11, 2001. Some time-urgent crises such as 9/11 are important; others are minor storms that "titillate the press, galvanize the opposition, and exercise the public before the storm blows itself out." British observers speculated that Prime Minister Gordon Brown would be the equal of his predecessor Tony Blair in dealing with "unexpected events—from terrorist attacks to emergency summits," but were concerned about whether his careful and serious style would allow him to adapt well to less important but politically fraught crises.[47]

Time-urgent crises are accompanied by individual and organizational stress. For individuals, the typical pattern is an increase in adrenalin and other hormonal flows that may improve alertness and energy levels. But the role of stress follows the curve of an inverted U: past an optimal point, distraction and fatigue can interfere with reasoning.[48] Organizations also respond to stress. Standard operating procedures may be relaxed by the sense of crisis, but an extreme relaxation of routine can destroy organizational effectiveness.[49]

We can make a distinction between routine and novel crises. A moderate earthquake in California and a Level 3 hurricane in Florida are routine crises. Systems are in place to deal with them; trained practitioners have built up an intuitive tacit knowledge of how to respond based on years of experience, and their organizational routines prove well adapted to the needs of the situation. Studies of airline pilots show that because flying procedures are so standardized and technologically controlled, the performance of cockpit crews is little affected by differences in captains under normal circumstances. "The time when Captain's leadership makes a big difference in crew performance is when things go wrong—for example, a non-routine mechanical problem, the need to divert to an unfamiliar airport in deteriorating weather, and so on."[50]

Hurricane Katrina in 2005 and the 2004 South Asian tsunami were novel in their scale and overwhelmed existing organizational responses. Sometimes prepared routines can be counterproductive in novel situations. New York firefighters "heroically fought the fires in the Twin Towers simply as an enlarged version of a skyscraper fire. They missed the novelty of the structural damage high up that would fairly rapidly lead to the collapse of the buildings." Leonard and Howitt point out that in routine crises, the most appropriate leadership is a command-and-control approach that implements a hierarchical system of general approaches and applies them to the specific situation. But in novel crises, an appropriate leadership style involves a muted command presence and a flatter horizontal structure that produces collaboration in developing understanding and design for a new approach. Such situations require expertise in adaptive leadership. Leonard and Howitt divide leadership in urgent crises into three phases: understanding, design, and execution. Authority and hierarchy are appropriate for all three phases of routine crises, but only for the third phase of novel crises.[51]

Howitt and Leonard also point out that there are three quite different types of work that need to be performed in a major crisis.[52] Cognitive work by analysts can help to diagnose the situation; operational work requires tacit knowledge and experience more than analysis; and political work by top leaders requires strategic choices as well as managing relations with the outside environment, such as the press and the public. A successful leader in a crisis has to have the contextual intelligence to know which decisions to make and which to leave to others. When Baltimore suffered a severe fire in a train tunnel, Mayor Martin O'Malley successfully managed the crisis by delegating key decisions to the operators. After the attack on the World Trade Center in New York, Mayor Giuliani's success as a leader was not through becoming involved in detailed operations, but in the public work of providing crucial reassurance to a confused and terrified public.

Effective crisis leadership is not merely a matter of understanding when to delegate decisions and how to reassure the public. It also involves precrisis leadership in building a system, training and preparing in advance. In other words, transactional management skills are essential, not just soft power reassurance after the crisis strikes. For example, many observers have criticized the absence of top leadership in managing operations and providing reassurance when Hurricane Katrina struck New Orleans in 2005. But the crisis leadership failures began long before the storm came ashore.

INFORMATION FLOWS

Shaping the context of information flows is an important part of effective leadership at all levels. Chester Barnard, an astute chief executive of AT&T, pointed out long ago that every group or organization has both a formal and an informal system of information flows.[53] Orders flow down the formal chain of command and reports flow back up. But in practice, some of the most important information flows circumvent and supplement the formal flow or are lateral communications among followers. Gossip is rarely idle; it makes groups work. Government produces reams of paper, but in its most important communications it is often an oral culture.

Understanding and shaping information flows is important in the leadership of small groups as well as large organizations. Richard Hackman's studies of teams found that the most important feature predicting success was getting teams set up right in the first place and creating a group culture of communication and information. Leaders then needed to monitor and maintain the teams and to learn at what stages of their work coaching could provide useful information.[54]

Leaders need to understand how to design and monitor effective information systems to implement their plans. Leaders who are not aware of the context of how information reaches them are likely to be told and believe what followers think the leaders want to hear. An emperor need not wait for a young boy to say he has no clothes; he can build such warning points into the system. When military leaders told President Bush they had all the troops they needed in Iraq, he probably did not discount what he heard as coming out of the climate of fear that Secretary of Defense Rumsfeld had created among the military officers in the Pentagon. Leaders can also be cross-examiners who push back on the information they receive. When they do not, as Kenneth Lay found out at Enron, the result can be disastrous. When Heinrich von Pierer lost his job as the head of Siemens in 2007, he denied any personal involvement in the company's bribery, but "the fact that so much of it occurred under his watch has raised questions about his management."[55]

Leaders need to be aware of the changing context of how they receive and process unwelcome new information. Woodrow Wilson kept an open mind in the early stages of examining issues, but became more resistant to new information after he made up his mind on an issue. According to his closest advisor, "Once a decision is made, it is final. There is no moving him after that."[56] Similarly, Colin Powell's chief of staff described George W. Bush as "too aloof, too distant from the details of postwar planning once his mind was made up. Underlings exploited Bush's detachment."[57]

Franklin Roosevelt described his own style as "political juggling." He kept himself in the center of information flows by playing off one advisor against another. This was effective for a one-way flow of inputs to the president that ensured his control, but his failure to inform subordinates made for an inefficient process in which there was inadequate outward flow of information needed to allow his subordinates to do their work effectively. For example, his secretary of state was not included or informed of his meetings with Stalin and Churchill at Yalta.

Leaders also need to understand how the information they provide will travel and be interpreted by followers. Distortion and exaggeration will vary with situations. When a king says, "Who will rid me of this troublesome priest?" he may or may not mean to convey an order and a death sentence, but he should understand the difference. When guards at Abu Ghraib are told to "soften these detainees up for interrogation," they may not hear the fine print of constraints that leaders may (or may not) have intended to convey.

The military acronym KISS—Keep it simple, stupid—pays tribute to the way complicated or ill-formed orders can be distorted by the contexts of information flows. As two combat-experienced generals commented about a 2007 presidential debate in which political candidates made light of such concerns, "Complex situational ethics cannot be applied during the stress of combat. The rules must be firm and absolute; if torture is broached as a possibility, it will become a reality. This has had disastrous consequences."[58] And when there is no accountability at the top, that information flows quickly to the followers. As the former chief legal officer of GE concludes, "There is no more important task for the CEO than demonstrating that the top executives will be held just as accountable for lapses in integrity as they are for missing their numbers—and that the generals will be held to higher standards than the troops."[59] We turn to these questions of integrity and the relationship between effective and ethical leadership in the concluding chapter.

FIVE

Good and Bad Leaders

Heroes lack blemish, but leaders have warts. Rare is the leader without flaws. David defeated Goliath and saved Israel, but later, as king, he seduced Bathsheba and deliberately sent her husband to certain death in battle.[1] Leaders are all too human. Sometimes good people do bad things, and vice versa.

Leadership involves the use of power, and as Lord Acton famously warned, power corrupts. Yet without power leaders cannot lead. In studying managers, David C. McClelland and David H. Burnham distinguished three motivational groups of people: those who care most about doing something better have a "need for achievement"; those who think most about friendly relations with others have a "need for affiliation"; and those who care most about having an impact on others show a "need for power." They found that the third group turned out to be the most effective leaders, but they cautioned that "power motivation refers not to dictatorial behavior but to a desire to have an impact, to be strong and influential." Emotional maturity and training are important means of limiting a narcissistic lust for power.[2] In their view, ethics and power can be mutually reinforcing rather than in conflict.

Machiavelli also addressed the importance of ethics for leaders, but primarily in terms of the impression that apparent virtue makes on followers. The appearance of virtue is an important source of a leader's soft power. Of the virtues a prince should have, Machiavelli wrote that "it is most essential that he should seem to have them; I will even venture to affirm that if he has and invariably practices them all, they are hurtful, while the appearance of having them is useful."[3] As we saw earlier, Machiavelli also stressed the importance of hard power when a leader faces a trade-off with soft power, "since being loved depends upon his subjects, while his being feared depends upon himself." Machiavelli believed that when one has to choose, it is better to be feared than to be loved, but he also understood that fear and love are not opposites.

The anarchic world of Italian Renaissance city states was more violent and dangerous than the twentieth-century organizations studied by McClelland and Burnham, but elements of Machiavelli's advice remain relevant to modern leaders. As we saw earlier, "bullies with a vision" can succeed in modern organizations. In addition to the courage of the lion, Machiavelli also extolled the strategic deceptiveness of the fox. As Joseph Badaracco, who teaches ethics at Harvard Business School, says, "Idealism untempered by realism often does little to improve the world." He recounts the fox-like strategy of Dr. Edouard Sakiz, CEO of Roussel Uclaf, a French pharmaceutical company that had to decide whether to market the abortion drug RU 486. Sakiz faced strong opposition from his German parent company and from antiabortion groups. By appearing to cancel the drug, Sakiz mobilized the support of pro-abortion groups and the French Health Ministry. He then announced that Roussel Uclaf would reverse its decision and market the drug after all. "He had used the predictable responses of the many stakeholders to orchestrate a series of events that helped achieve his ends, without looking like he was leading the way. In fact, it appeared as if he were giving in to outside pressure."[4] Some would call Sakiz a good leader and others would not, but none could doubt that his deceptive strategy was effective.

DEFINING GOOD AND BAD

One of the problems in identifying good and bad leaders is the ambiguous ways in which people use the word "good." It is sometimes used to mean "ethical" and sometimes to mean "effective." As we saw earlier, some leadership theorists build both meanings into their concept by defining leaders as those who produce positive change for a group. Thus leadership is ethical by definition, and someone like Hitler is a mere power wielder, not a leader.[5] I think it helps to keep the two meanings of "good" separate. A good knife is one that cuts sharply whether it is misused or not. A good thief steals without getting caught; if, like Robin Hood, he shares part of his booty with the poor, some may see him as good in the ethical as well the effective sense. A good leader is one who effectively helps a group to create and achieve objectives for better or worse. Thus Hitler was an effective leader with morally bad purposes for his first decade in power. In the end, because he led his followers to disaster, he turned out to be a bad leader in both the moral and the effective sense.

In practice, we can judge both effectiveness and ethics in three dimensions: goals, means, and consequences. Effective goals combine realism and risk in a vision that can be implemented, whereas ethical goals are judged by the morality of the intentions and vision. Good goals have to meet our moral standards, as well as a feasibility test. Effective means are those that are efficient for achieving the goals, but ethical means depend on the quality, not the efficiency, of the approaches employed. A leader's consequential effectiveness involves achieving the group's goals, but ethical consequences mean good results not just for the in-group, but for outsiders as well. These dimensions are summed up in Table 5.1. Of course in practice, the two dimensions are often closely related. A leader who pursues unrealistic (ineffective) goals or uses ineffective means can produce terrible moral consequences for followers. Thus reckless reality testing that leads to immoral consequences can become an ethical failure. Conversely, a leader's good intentions are not proof of what is sometimes misleadingly called "moral clarity." For example, those who justify the invasion of Iraq because it was intended to remove a brutal dictator are practicing one-dimensional moral judgment.

It is easy to vilify leaders who are truly bad in both senses of the word outlined in Table 5.1. Saddam Hussein attracted real constituents and tried to build Iraqi nationhood, but he was brutal and impetuous and brought great harm to his people. When asked why he invaded Kuwait, he replied, "When I get something into my head I act. That's just the way I am." Slobodan Milosevic plundered state coffers, played upon nationalist fears and ambitions, and butchered his neighbors, and every war he fought left the Serbs

TABLE 5.1   Two Meanings of Good Leadership

"Good" =	Effective	Ethical
Goals	Balance of realism and risk in vision	Values of intentions, goals
Means	Efficiency of means to ends	Quality of means used
Consequences	Success in achieving group's goals	Good results for in-group and for outsiders

worse off. "Yugoslavia had no right to expect a Nelson Mandela in 1989. But all it needed was a leader with decent instincts and abilities. Instead it got a monster."[6] Sapamurat Niyazov, the first president of independent Turkmenistan, restricted travel, free speech, public assembly, fair elections, and independent media, and his "perceived enemies disappeared into psychiatric wards or jails." Nonetheless, he built huge self-glorifying monuments and called himself the father of his people.[7]

Alas, the list of bad leaders goes on and on, and they come in many varieties, not all as dramatic as the monsters just described.[8] Looking at other recent bad leaders, Barbara Kellerman found three types of ineffective leadership even among those who initially succeeded. Juan Samaranch, for example, was incompetent and lost effectiveness in managing the International Olympic Committee. Others were too rigid to be effective, such as Mary Meeker, a Wall Street analyst who rode the upswing of the market for dotcom stocks in the 1990s but could not adjust to the downturn.[9] A third type of ineffectiveness, intemperance, is illustrated by Boris Yeltsin, who was a hero when he stood on a tank to resist a coup against the Russian government, but whose fondness for drink later undercut his effectiveness as president.

Four other categories of bad leadership represent unethical practices. "Chainsaw" Al Dunlap of the Sunbeam Corporation was callous in the way he treated employees, associates, and stockholders. William Aramony, who stole from the United Way, was corrupt. Radovan Karadzic of Bosnia was an evil leader because he enjoyed harming people. Kellerman accuses Bill Clinton of insularity, or thinking only of his own group, because he failed to respond to the genocide in Rwanda.[10] I will challenge this last judgment later, but the important point now is that one can imagine many types of bad leadership.

Leaders' ethical lapses can occur in different ways at different stages of their careers. Sometimes competitive pressures cause leaders to abandon their principles; then they become destructive achievers. Others, however, suffer from the Bathsheba syndrome: they rise by ethical means but find that success produces complacency, hubris, and a sense of privileged access. Their failure to observe the impartial standards of ethical behavior may be more than just egoistic lapses or succumbing to temptation. It may also involve a cognitive dimension in which leaders do not think that impartial ethical standards apply to them because they are leaders. That is often reinforced by the special deference with which followers treat them. As one expert put it, "The justificatory force of leadership induces and maintains a leader's belief that he or she is removed from the scope of morality. Although the leader recognizes the general force of moral requirements as they are applied to others, he or she may fail to see that these requirements apply to him or her as well."[11] David understood that what he did was wrong; he just did not think the restrictions applied to him. That raises the larger question of whether leaders should be held to the same moral standards as ordinary people.

PUBLIC AND PRIVATE MORALITY

During the debate over his impeachment, many of President Clinton's opponents argued that his deceptive liaison with a White House intern showed a flawed character that made him an unworthy leader.[12] His defenders responded that unlike Nixon, Clinton performed well in his public role as president, and his sexual behavior (and lies about an extramarital affair) was a private matter. Public and private morality should be kept separate, they said. French observers, long used to this distinction, were amused by the Puritanism of the American debate. Few seemed scandalized when a mistress and illegitimate daughter as well as a wife appeared at the funeral of French President François Mitterrand. Aside from sexual temptations, there is a more serious question about the separation of public and private morality. Should leaders be held to a different standard? Take the biblical injunction "Thou shalt not kill." When choosing a roommate or spouse, that commandment would rank high on the list of desired moral values. At the same time, most people would not vote for an absolute pacifist to become president of their country. Presidents have a fiduciary obligation to protect the people who elected them, and under certain circumstances, that may involve ordering troops into battle to take lives. In their private capacity, such leaders are held to common moral standards. In democracies, at least, their personal acts are punishable by law as well as by loss of followers' trust. A president who killed an intern could be impeached, tried, and jailed. On the other hand, the role of a public leader may require a president to overcome a private aversion to taking human life. Even in less dramatic circumstances, followers want leaders to protect and advance their interests even if doing so involves deception. Up to a point, they want leaders to sacrifice their personal scruples and depart from everyday moral rules in order to advance the group interest. As for justice, experimenters have found that people "preferred ingroup-favoring leaders over fair ones."[13]

The resulting dilemma for leaders is called the problem of "dirty hands."[14] To advance the interests of the group for whom they have a fiduciary responsibility, leaders may have to do things they would not be willing to do in their private lives. As trustees, they have an additional set of moral obligations.[15] The political philosopher Michael Walzer argues that if it is right for a leader to try to succeed, "then it must also be right to get one's hands dirty. But one's hands get dirty from doing what it is wrong to do."[16] Walzer uses the example of a leader who orders a man tortured to discover the location of a terrorist bomb in a city and prevent the loss of innocent life even though he personally believes torture is wrong.[17] Sometimes, leaders can maintain their conscience and sense of integrity by distinguishing between the public and private spheres. Thus Mario Cuomo, the Catholic governor of New York, personally opposed abortion but argued eloquently that in his role as governor, he was obligated to think of the requirements of a public official in a pluralistic democracy. By keeping the public and private spheres separate, he avoided a sense of dirty hands. Sometimes, however, there are two equally compelling standards in the same public sphere, and the problem of dirty hands is unavoidable.[18]

Max Weber famously distinguished an ethic of ultimate ends from an ethic of responsibility. In the former, absolute moral imperatives must not be violated for the sake of good consequences, but an ethic of responsibility must focus on the results. Weber warns that "he who seeks the salvation of the soul, his own soul and others, should not seek it along the avenue of politics."[19] In the philosophical traditions of the Western Enlightenment, ethicists distinguish a deontological or rule-based approach associated with Immanuel Kant from a consequentialist approach associated with utilitarians such as Jeremy Bentham and John Stuart Mill. The two traditions each provide an important strand of contemporary moral rules in the West today.

The difference can be illustrated by a simple story.[20] Imagine you are an observer for an NGO in Darfur and you come across a village where a military commander has lined up fifty people against a wall and is about to execute them because someone from the village fired a shot that killed a soldier last night. You say, "Stop! Only one shot was fired, and thus most of these people are innocent." The commander looks at you with disdain and hands you a rifle, saying that if you kill one person, he will let the rest go.

He warns you not to try anything foolish because his soldiers now have their guns trained on you. Do you fire and save forty-nine lives, thus dirtying your hands, or do you drop the rifle and maintain the integrity of your principles while watching the commander kill fifty people? As the example changes to killing one innocent person to save millions, or to Walzer's ticking terrorist bomb, the trade-off between a leader's scruples and the consequences for followers makes the choice more difficult for many people.[21] At what price does personal integrity translate into selfishness and a violation of followers' trust?

There are no easy answers to such problems, and recent scientific discoveries suggest that evolution may have hardwired different solutions to the dilemma into the human brain. Another classic philosophers' case contrasts how people respond to a runaway trolley car. In one case, you can push someone into the path of the car so that it slows sufficiently to allow five people to escape it. In another case, you can throw a switch that sends the car down a track that kills one person rather than another track where it would kill five. The outcome in lives is the same in either case— one person dies or five die—but most people recoil from the first action more than the second. A recent study has shown that people with damage to the ventromedial prefrontal cortex region of the brain are about twice as likely to push someone in front of the train or suffocate a baby whose crying would reveal to enemy soldiers where a family is hiding. Harvard philosopher Joshua Greene concludes, "I think it's very convincing now that there are at least two systems working when we make moral judgments. There's an emotional system that depends on this specific part of the brain, and another system that performs more utilitarian cost-benefit analyses which in these people is clearly intact."[22] The experiment suggests that "the decision on how to act is not a single, rational calculation of the sort that moral philosophers have generally assumed is going on, but a conflict between two processes, with one (the emotional) sometimes able to override the other (the utilitarian, the location of which this study does not address)."[23]

Whatever the neuroscience, in daily practice, people's sense of moral obligation tends to come from three sources. One is a sense of conscience, which is personally or religiously informed and leads individuals to try to achieve a sense of moral integrity. A second involves rules of common morality that society treats as obligations for all individuals, and a third is codes of professional ethics and conventional expectations that might be considered the duties of one's role.[24] Leaders are subject to all three, and these sources of moral obligation are frequently in tension with each other. Often there is no single solution. As Isaiah Berlin once noted, because "the ends of men are many, and not all of them are in principle compatible with each other, then the possibility of conflict—and tragedy—can never wholly be eliminated from human life, either personal or social."[25]

We tend to make moral judgments in terms of the three dimensions of goals, means, and consequences, often with a delicate weighing of the trade-offs among them. Because of their special roles, we often put more weight on consequences when judging leaders. At the same time, if followers allow leaders to argue that the duties of their role require them to think only of consequences, they may slip into a self-justificatory style that too fully detaches them from other rules of moral behavior.

Conscience and the search for a sense of personal integrity can be an important limit on the slippery slope of such overly permissive morality. For example, Nixon once told an interviewer that his role justified his actions: "When the president does it, that means it is not illegal." That attitude led members of his inner circle to believe "that the president and those acting on his behalf could carry out illegal acts with impunity if they were convinced that the nation's security demanded it." But as one of those followers later said, "I finally realized that what had gone wrong in the Nixon White House was a meltdown in personal integrity. Without it, we failed to understand the constitutional limits on presidential power and comply with statutory law."[26] Similar questions have arisen about the interpretation of executive power by President Bush and Vice President Cheney in the struggle against terrorism.

Mindless adherence to society's rules is not the same as integrity. As Hannah Arendt described Adolf Eichmann, "In one respect, Eichmann did indeed follow Kant's precepts: a law was a law, there could be no exceptions. . . . No exceptions—this was the proof that he had always acted against his 'inclinations,' whether they were sentimental or inspired by interest, that he had always done his 'duty.'"[27] To take another example, in *The Adventures of Huckleberry Finn*, Mark Twain has his hero help his slave friend Jim run away even though Huck feels guilty about breaking the law. Conscience and integrity may sometimes require violating rules and laws when the alternative is highly immoral consequences.

Some leaders solve such conflicts with "sleep test ethics" as their sign of integrity: an act is right if you can sleep with the results.[28] But the danger of such tests is "me-ism," or the absence of any larger standards to control the ego. If leaders develop ingrained moral habits that are something like Aristotle's classical virtues of character—courage, justice, prudence, and temperance—the dangers of ego-centered intuitionism become less acute. But different cultures and groups shape character in different ways, and so moral intuitions are not all the same; a virtuous character in some cultures would not seem so in another. Osama bin Laden developed a character and a religious sense of justice that allowed him to commit what we see as mass murder, but it probably also allowed him to sleep soundly after September 11, 2001.

Many societies have ethical systems that stress impartiality and have an analogue to the golden rule: Do unto others as you would have them do unto you. Your interests and my interests should be treated the same way. However, appealing to an intuitive sense of fairness—treating others as you would want to be treated, not playing favorites, and being sensible to individual needs—does not always provide a solution. Imagine a parent with one flute and three children, each of whom wants it.[29] The first child says, "I made it"; the second says, "I am the only one who can play it"; and the third says, "I have no other toys." Even with a thought experiment about deciding behind a veil of ignorance, the principle of justice as fairness remains unclear in some cases. In such instances, the parent (or leader) may find it more appropriate to turn to a procedural or institutional solution in which the children bargain with each other or agree on a lottery or on a neutral figure to decide how time with the flute will be allocated or shared. The parent can also teach or coach the children about sharing, which is a different image of leadership as persuasion rather than exercise of authority. Developing intuitions about process and institutions—helping a group decide how to decide—is often one of the most important moral roles that leaders (and parents) play. As we saw earlier, suppressing conflict may lead to worse consequences in a group than if a leader helps to orchestrate and moderate multiparty conflict so that followers learn new behavior.

SELF-SERVING VERSUS GROUP-SERVING DECEPTION

Sometimes leaders have different objectives from those of a large part of their group, and rather than reveal the differences, they deceive their followers. When such actions are self-serving, as in cases of corruption or narcissistic ego gratification, moral censure is easy. Jim Jones of the Peoples Temple was such a case. Other leaders have objectives different from their followers', and they invest heavily and successfully in educating the group to a different point of view. They transform their followers' moral choices and we tend to praise them.

In other instances, however, leaders find it impossible to educate their followers adequately in time, or followers are too deeply divided to reach a consensus that will sustain group action. In such circumstances, some leaders may take a paternalist view and decide to deceive their followers for what they see as their followers' larger or later good. For example, as discussed earlier, Lyndon Johnson deceived his southern supporters in order to pass the 1957 Civil Rights Act. Charles de Gaulle did not reveal his strategy for Algerian independence when he came to power in 1958 because he knew that would doom it to failure. John F. Kennedy misled the public about the role of Turkish missiles in the deal that ended the Cuban Missile Crisis in 1962.[30] Franklin Roosevelt lied to the American public about a German attack on an American destroyer in an effort to overcome isolationist resistance to helping Britain before World War II. And Winston Churchill, a paragon of twentieth-century leadership, once said that the truth may be "so precious that she should always be attended by a bodyguard of lies."[31]

The fact that consequences may sometimes justify leaders' violation of norms about honest means does not signify that all lies are equal, or that we must suspend moral judgment in such cases. Machiavellian deception is often part of a strategy, for example, in bargaining to get a deal or even in bringing a group to accept new goals. But intentions matter. Deception that is purely self-serving turns from a strategy that may benefit others into selfish manipulation of others. Even if one admits that deception may sometimes be necessary, one can still ask about the importance of the goal, the availability of alternative means to achieve that goal, whether the deception can be contained or is likely to spread through precedent or example, the damage done to various victims of the deception, and the accountability of the deceivers (whether it can be discovered and explained later).[32] One study concludes that presidential lies "inevitably turn into monsters that strangle their creators."[33] Whether true or not, it is all too easy for leaders to think they are telling a noble lie for the good of their followers when they are merely lying for political or personal convenience. That makes it all the more important that we subject to moral discourse the nature of the trade-offs that leaders make between their ends and means.

Geoff Mulgan, an advisor to Tony Blair, wrote, "Our best guarantees that rulers will act morally come less from imposing rigid rules and more from establishing powerful ways to call them into account so that others can judge if their claims are self-serving. Here there has been much progress with the spread of inquiries and commissions . . . that can examine decisions and help the public to make rounded judgments." Democracy can help because widespread experience of power keeps government honest. "Too much centralization and too much power in the hands of technocrats and managers leave the public detached, disengaged and prone to oscillate between excessive identification with leaders and excessive contempt: between populism and cynicism."[34] Even putting aside questions of political ideology, a democratic process is a pragmatic way to ensure that modern leaders enter their position with a firm claim of legitimacy and can be held accountable once they get there.[35] The answer to some of the hard questions about judging good and bad leaders turns on institutions.

COSTS, RISKS, AND LUCK

Even when we judge leaders by their consequences, we can still make moral judgments about how leaders distribute the risks and costs of their actions. As we saw in chapter 4, in deciding how to decide, a leader may choose an efficient autocratic approach or a more participatory approach. The decision can be judged not only on effectiveness, but it also has an ethical component if it leads to learning by the group. There are also questions of how risk is allocated. Ernest Shackleton, the early twentieth-century polar explorer, is described in case studies as a great leader because of the way he kept his men working together after the ice had crushed their ship, but few of the cases examine whether he should have put them in such a risky situation in the first place. Rash assessments of reality that impose high risks on others can be condemned on moral as well as effectiveness terms. People who try to climb Mt. Everest accept a degree of risk, but a team leader still has to make sure that the whole group understands the balance between risk and achievement.[36] It is one thing to pose a grand vision that leads people up a mountain; it is another to lead them too close to the edge of a cliff.

Finally, when justifying leaders' actions by their consequences, there is the question of costs imposed on others and the issue of what the philosopher Bernard Williams called "moral luck." Many a leader, including secular saints like Gandhi, have imposed enormous costs on their spouse and children that would be condemned if carried out by your next-door neighbor but are exonerated because of their subsequent accomplishments. Williams points out that the painter Paul Gauguin deserted his family to travel to Tahiti. The result was the creation of some of the world's finest art, and many see the consequences as justifying his mistreatment of his family. Yet if Gauguin's ship had sunk en route to Tahiti, he would be remembered primarily as a callous man who deserted his family. Williams argues that it matters how intrinsic the cause of the failure is to the project itself. A shipwreck would be "too external to unjustify him, something which only his failure as a painter can do."[37] Some dimensions of luck are purely fortuitous. Machiavelli warned of the role of *fortuna*, but people can also help to make their luck. Reckless reality-testing and unnecessary risk-taking may be part of "bad luck." Conversely, many sports teams practice and analyze their opponent's game so that they can capitalize on errors and benefit from "good luck." Because we weigh consequences more heavily in our moral judgment of leaders, history tends to be kind to the lucky and unkind to the unlucky, but we can still judge them in terms of the means they used and the causes of their luck.

That still leaves open the question of what is the appropriate point at which to judge leaders. Failures at one point in history may look more successful at a later time. Woodrow Wilson was unlucky that a stroke crippled him in the midst of his campaign to educate the public about the League of Nations. Ironically, had the stroke killed rather than crippled him, it is likely that the Senate would have ratified a version of the League, and Wilson's place in history as a transformational leader would have been more secure. A British politician once wrote that "all political lives, unless they are cut off in midstream at a happy juncture, end in failure."[38] Another observer notes, "Politics has its own automatic stabilizers. Leaders start out with the benefit of the doubt," but after a decade or thereabouts, "democracy demands changes. Scores of promises will necessarily have been broken over such a span. Politicians who once seemed driven by ideals are tarnished by the grubby compromises of power."[39] One of the hard choices for leaders is to know when to relinquish power. Time may be unkind, but it helps to go out at the top of your game.

President George W. Bush likes to compare himself to Harry Truman, who left office with low popularity rankings because of the stalemated Korean War but later recovered in public esteem. Some historians doubt history will be as kind to Bush because Truman's role in fostering European recovery and building the NATO alliance were seen as solid accomplishments at that time, whereas "Bush, by contrast, lacks any success of comparable magnitude to compensate for his mismanagement of the Iraq war."[40] Far from being beleaguered by the war, however, Bush is reported to be self-confident and perseveres because of his "unconquerable faith in the rightness of his Big Idea" that history is moving toward democracy. "I believe a gift of that Almighty to all is freedom," he says.[41] Whether the loftiness of his vision and his analysis of the context have led people up the mountain or over a cliff remains to be seen. Truman's biographer David McCullough suggests that "about 50 years has to go by before you can appraise a presidency—the dust has to settle."[42] At this point, however, the odds for Bush do not look favorable.[43]

Even over long periods, ratings of presidential greatness are not completely stable in public opinion. For example, one poll showed Kennedy outranking Franklin Roosevelt in 2002 and 2006, despite Kennedy's more modest accomplishments.[44] Maybe Teddy Roosevelt was lucky that the fourth place on Mount Rushmore was carved into stone before his higher ranking cousin Franklin entered office.[45]

THE ETHICS OF TRANSFORMATIONAL AND TRANSACTIONAL LEADERSHIP

Transactional leaders approach followers with an eye to exchanging one thing for another. Transforming leaders "engage with others in such a way that leaders and followers raise one another to higher levels of motivation and morality.... Perhaps the best modern example is Gandhi, who aroused and elevated the hopes and demands of millions of Indians and whose life and personality were enhanced in the process."[46] Because of this classic definition, many people assume that leaders with transformational objectives and an inspirational style are better or more ethical than leaders with more modest objectives and a transactional style. But the answer is more complex. Sometimes they are better, but sometimes they are worse.

Morally good and consequentially effective transformational leaders provide an inspiring vision of goals that overcomes self-interest and unites groups around common purposes. Their appeal to larger collective causes can overcome narrow factionalism in organizations and nations. Some theorists prefer transformational leaders because they develop and encourage new and broader energies among followers, while the performance gains of trans-actional leaders are likely to be more limited. Groups and nations that are rent by cleavages and factions can benefit from a leader who expresses objectives that encourage them to raise their sights to a common cause.

Common causes, however, are not always more moral than individual interests. Transformational leaders appeal to people's higher needs, but it is often not clear which needs are higher. Individual interests are not automatically less legitimate than collective ends. If a government official chooses to go to his daughter's softball game on a Saturday afternoon rather than serve the public interest by working in the office, which is the higher need? When the transformational leader Mao Tse-tung rallied the Chinese people around collective interests in the Great Leap Forward of the 1950s and the Cultural Revolution of the 1960s, the result was millions of unnecessary deaths. Transformation is not necessarily good.

Two centuries ago, the newly independent American colonists had a leader in George Washington, whose transformational objectives and inspirational skills proved essential for winning the war for independence from Great Britain. Nonetheless, they invented a very different type of institutional leadership when James Madison and other transactional leaders negotiated the Constitution and later explained it in the *Federalist Papers.* "Madison concentrated on a fact about human motivation that proves troublesome for transformational leadership theories: Not everyone is attracted to the same goals or leaders. . . . If transformational leaders are not able to persuade *everyone* to voluntarily accept a common vision, what is the likely status of people who prefer their own goals and visions?"[47]

Madison's famous solution to the problem of cleavage and faction in objectives was not to overcome division and conflict by trying to convert everyone to a common cause, but to overcome divisions by creating an institutional framework in which ambition countered ambition and faction countered faction. Separation of powers, checks and balances, and a decentralized federal system placed the emphasis on laws more than leaders. "Madisonian government works not because participants agree on goals, but because they can agree on specific activities (as in acts of legislation) that address their different goals. So too in 'private' organizations, like corporations, the glue that holds them together need not be consensus on ends but can be simply consent to means—agreement on rules, rights, and responsibilities that serve the separate interests of their participants."[48] Even when a group cannot agree on its ultimate goals, its members may be able to agree on means that create diversity and pluralism without destroying the group. In such circumstances, transactional leadership may be better than inspirational efforts at transformational leadership.

LEADERS AND INSTITUTIONS

The Madisonian example suggests that judging ethical leadership must include consideration of institutions. As one study of business leaders concludes, "Leadership ethical lapses are not due exclusively to the character and actions of leaders themselves."[49] Institutions such as boards of directors, shareholder committees, laws, and codes of conduct also matter. As we saw earlier, one of the key roles of leaders is the creation, maintenance, or change of institutions. For better and worse, both transactional and transformational leaders can undercut or destroy institutions. Machiavellian transactional leaders "know how to circumvent organizational systems in order to achieve their personal objectives and make political gains."[50] And as Max Weber pointed out a century ago, the charisma of inspirational leaders, which focuses authority in the individual, is a powerful solvent of institutions.

Institutions create constraints that sometimes hamper achievement of group goals. Madisonian government was not designed for efficiency. Law is often called "the wise restraints that make men free," but sometimes laws must be changed or broken, as the civil rights movement of the 1960s demonstrated. On an everyday level, whistle-blowers can play a disruptive but useful role in large bureaucracies, and a smart leader will find ways to protect them or channel their information into institutions such as ombudspersons. An inspirational leader who ignores institutions or breaks them must carefully consider the long-term ethical consequences as well as the immediate gains for the group.

As we saw earlier, one of the most important skills of good leaders is to design and maintain systems and institutions. This has both an effectiveness and an ethical component. Poorly designed institutions are those that fail to achieve a group's purpose, not in each particular instance but over the long term. Well-designed institutions include means for self-correction as well as ways of constraining the failures of leaders.[51] As the top legal officer of a major multinational corporation put it, "Ultimately, it is a company's culture that sustains high performance with high integrity." A leader needs to create an institutional framework in which "the company's norms and values are so widely shared and its reputation for integrity is so strong that most leaders and employees want to win the right way."[52]

Poorly designed or led institutions can also lead people astray. Obedience to institutional authority can be bad at times. Several decades ago, a famous experiment at Yale encouraged students to administer simulated brutal electrical shocks to their colleagues, and a simulated prison experiment at Stanford also demonstrated the capacity of intelligent people to submit blindly to authority. The very real recent case of Abu Ghraib Prison reminds us of both the importance and the danger of poorly designed institutions. The Abu Ghraib guards were reservists without special training who lacked supervision and were given the task of softening up detainees. It is not surprising that the result was various forms of torture.[53] The moral flaws were not only in the prison guards, but also in the higher level guardians who created and failed to monitor a flawed institutional framework. Good leadership is not merely inspiring people with a noble vision, but involves creating and maintaining the systems and institutions that allow effective and moral implementation.

MEANING AND IDENTITIES

This focus on institutions is not a denial of the importance of inspirational leadership. Leaders can be judged not only on their effectiveness in achieving group goals, but also on the meaning that they create and teach to their followers.[54] Leaders who are strong in "sense-making" are those who "know how to quickly capture the complexities of their environment and explain them to others in simple terms. This helps ensure that everyone is working from the same map."[55] Stanley Hoffmann, a leading authority on France, points to the important example of de Gaulle: "There is no exact equivalent for the word 'leadership' in French. . . . For the French, leadership means pedagogy: the capacity to explain the world, and to make people feel that the leadership takes them seriously. We haven't had a real teacher since de Gaulle, and that has produced a funk in France."[56] Inspirational leaders often use periods of crisis as teaching moments to educate their followers about new perspectives and the need for change. They create a narrative that gives meaning to the situation in which their followers find themselves. As the leaders provide meaning and identity they generate trust, which facilitates action by the group. Some groups may seek to preserve a tradition, and an inspirational conservative leader may help them maintain the status quo and give it meaning. Transformational leaders, by definition, seek change, and sometimes groups are in desperate need of change. As we have seen, change is not always good, and some transformational leaders, such as Hitler and Cambodia's Pol Pot, produced change with evil consequences.

Nonetheless, inspirational leaders with transformational goals have often played major roles in history. The world would be a poorer place without such leaders as Gandhi, Mandela, and King. King was brilliant at using soft power to "invert the resources of his opponents" by using nonviolence in the face of police brutality. His greatest skill was "the art of persuasive communication. He certainly had no riches or material rewards to offer his supporters—but he did have an honorable goal."[57] He used it effectively to mobilize and inspire common meaning for divergent groups who initially approached civil rights in different ways.

He did not start the civil rights movement and was not its only significant leader, but he was able to crystallize broader feelings about the need for social change in a way that improved rather than destroyed an institutional framework. Striking the right balance between existing institutions and changes in meaning is an important ethical task for leaders.

One of the most important ways leaders produce meaning is by establishing or changing a group's identity: "Leaders must be entrepreneurs of identity. The success of their leadership hinges on an ability to turn 'me' and 'you' into 'us.' "[58] It is far easier to reinforce the status quo than to change identity, yet the moral implications can be immense. Most leaders feed upon the existing identity and solidarity of their groups. In that sense they are insular and define their responsibilities to their group in a traditional manner. But some leaders see moral obligations beyond their immediate group and take actions to educate their followers about them. For example, Mandela could easily have chosen to define his group as black South Africans and sought revenge for the injustice of decades of apartheid and his own imprisonment. Instead, he worked tirelessly to expand the identity of his followers both by words and deeds. In one important symbolic gesture, he appeared at a rugby game wearing the jersey of the South African Springboks, a team that had previously signified white South African nationalism.[59] He seized the teaching moment at the end of apartheid.

After World War II, during which Germany had invaded France for the third time in seventy years, the diplomat Jean Monnet decided that revenge upon a defeated Germany would produce yet another tragedy and instead invented a plan for the gradual development of a European coal and steel community that eventually evolved into today's European Union. European integration has now helped to make war between France and Germany virtually unthinkable. Monnet used the moment of Europe's exhaustion not only to propose a larger vision but also to devise a successful transactional plan for its incremental implementation. Monnet was aided by the fact that the three postwar leaders of France, Germany, and Italy—Robert Schuman, Konrad Adenauer, and Alcide De Gasperi—had each been born in parts of their country that had once been under foreign jurisdiction and were unusually amenable to seeing national identity in a broader European context. As the psychologist Howard Gardner concludes, "The heroes of my study turn out to be Mahatma Gandhi and Jean Monnet, two men who attempted to enlarge the sense of 'we.' Monnet devoted his life to the proposition that Europe need not remain a set of battling nations. . . . Gandhi devoted his life to exemplifying the idea that individuals of different races and ethnicities need not oppose one another violently."[60]

Gandhi was not fully successful, however, in changing sectarian and communal identities in India. Two of his contemporaries (who, like Gandhi, started their careers as lawyers) took a different approach to group identities. Jawaharlal Nehru, focusing on the elite politics of creating an independent, democratic, and socialist India, made different choices from Gandhi's about educating the masses. Unlike his mentor, who believed that "independence would have to be grounded in a total moral transformation, Nehru was committed with equal conviction to making freedom a reality for all Indians through the exercise of state power."[61] Nehru sought a unified, democratic, and secular India; his competition, Mohammad Ali Jinnah, sought to create a separate nation of Pakistan for India's minority Muslims. The result was a partition that Gandhi opposed and that caused a million deaths and a legacy of enmity that resulted in three wars. "The only one who knew what was coming was Gandhi, mystic, genius and eccentric, who drove the other great men crazy by insisting on living among and ministering to the poor, the non-elite."[62] Six months after the independence of India and Pakistan, Gandhi was killed by a Hindu extremist who objected to his efforts to reconcile with Muslims. In India today, Nehru's influence is greater than Gandhi's, but in global terms, Gandhi has become the greater teacher and hero.

As we saw earlier, globalization is one of the important changes occurring in the macro-environment of leadership today. Making sense of intergroup relations in a global context poses a new set of ethical as well as effective problems for leaders. Traditionally, most leaders felt that their moral obligation was to their own group; they mobilized and articulated the needs and interests of their followers. As discussed earlier, when we look above the small group level, we can see that most human identities are "imagined communities."[63] Few people have direct experience of the other members of their community. For the past century or two, the nation has been the imagined community that people were willing to die for, and most leaders have seen their primary obligations as national.

In a world of globalization, many people belong to a number of imagined communities. Some—local, regional, national, cosmopolitan—seem to be arranged as concentric circles, where the strength of identity diminishes with distance, but in a global information age, this ordering has become confused. As we saw in chapter 2, many identities are like Venn diagrams of overlapping circles, which are sustained by the Internet and cheap travel. Diasporas are now connected across national borders; professional groups have transnational standards; activist groups ranging from environmentalists to terrorists also connect across borders. Sovereignty is no longer as absolute as it once seemed. The UN has recognized a responsibility to protect endangered peoples in sovereign states, even though the global community is wrestling with how to implement this new doctrine in places like Darfur. The question of whether a new generation of leaders will be better at coping with this new world is still an open one.

Earlier I noted that Barbara Kellerman accused Bill Clinton of insular leadership in failing to respond to the genocide in Rwanda in 1994. In one sense, she is right. But other leaders were also insular, and no nation responded adequately. Had Clinton tried to send U.S. troops he would have encountered stiff resistance in Congress. Particularly after the death of American soldiers in Somalia, his followers were not ready for another humanitarian intervention. Clinton has acknowledged that he could have done more to galvanize the UN and other nations to save some of the lives that were lost in Rwanda, but good leaders today are often caught between their cosmopolitan inclinations and their more traditional obligations to the followers who elected them.[64]

Insularity is not an all-or-nothing moral dimension. In a world in which people are organized in national communities, a purely cosmopolitan ideal is unrealistic.[65] A leader who claims there is an obligation to equalize incomes globally is not credible, but a leader who says that more should be done to reduce poverty and disease can rally followers. As the philosopher Kwame Anthony Appiah puts it, "Thou shalt not kill is a test you take pass-fail. Honor thy father and thy mother admits of gradations."[66] The same is true of cosmopolitanism versus insularity. We may admire leaders who make efforts to increase their followers' concern for the consequences of their actions on the out-group, but it does little good to hold them to an impossible standard whose pursuit could undercut their capacity to remain leaders.

THE MORALITY OF FOLLOWERS

Inspirational leaders can try to educate their followers, but like Gandhi, they may not fully succeed. We can also make moral judgments about their followers. A common saying is that people get the leaders they deserve. On this argument, the pervasive caste system in Indian society made Gandhi's task of reconciliation impossible; the authoritarian nature of Russian culture is bound to produce a czar or a Putin; British traditions since the Magna Carta make czars impossible; and the conformism of Japanese society makes charismatic leaders less likely there. Such cultural determinism is too simple—witness the changes in Germany over the past century—but it remains true that the moral choices that followers make can constrain even the most saintly of leaders. The old adage that people get the leaders they deserve is an oversimplification, but certainly bad followers help produce bad leaders and constrain good ones.

Some theorists talk about concentric circles of followers based on their level of engagement and loyalty to a leader: "isolates, bystanders, participants, activists, and diehards."[67] Others add a second dimension related to the followers' degree of independent thinking, ranging from dependent and compliant at one end of the spectrum to independent and critical at the other end. The combination of two dimensions of loyalty and independent thinking provides a normative grid for judging followers, as Table 5.2 illustrates.[68]

Theorists argue that the best followers are those who are empowered to think for themselves and who, though loyal, are willing to criticize and correct their leaders. Those who are passive do little to help the leaders achieve group goals. Conformists are loyal in pursuing the leader's goals, but fail to put necessary constraints on leaders and thus allow the group to pursue mistaken goals or use immoral means. Those who are critical but have low loyalty to the leader become alienated and also do not help to achieve group goals or to correct leaders' mistakes. In this view, independent thinkers with high loyalty are the best followers: leaders empower them, and they in turn empower their leaders in a social contract of trust that helps protect leaders from mistakes.[69]

TABLE 5.2   Good and Bad Followers

	Low Loyalty	High Loyalty
Independent thinking	Alienated	Empowered
Compliant thinking	Passive	Conformist

Trust arises from followers' experience with their leaders' ability, benevolence, and integrity, but negative experiences tend to weigh more heavily than positive ones.[70] That added costliness of mistakes makes the protective role of empowered followers all the more important. The difference can be summarized with an anecdote. One executive told another, "If I point my hand to the north and say 'Go,' four thousand employees will obediently march, even over a cliff." The second executive responded, "If I were to point my arm north and say 'Go,' four thousand hands would move my arm to the northeast or northwest so we avoid going over the cliff."[71]

Many leaders speak of empowerment of their followers but fail in its practice. For example, Nehru had a style in office that was not fully consistent with his democratic words. As a biographer describes India's first prime minister, "In the highest public office in the country he developed a vast and unsustainable public role for himself. He proved incapable of delegating authority and effectively sharing power among colleagues. . . . He did not nurture and encourage younger members of government unlike his own mentor, Gandhi. . . . He had made the role virtually impossible except for one like himself, a personality driven by vision and a sense of personal vocation and in a real sense an outsider to the grass-roots world of politics."[72] Nehru deserves credit for the fact that India is a democracy, but his legacy of empowering his followers is far from unblemished and remains the source of significant problems to this day.

As we saw in chapter 2, when followers are confronted with choices, they can take one of three basic approaches: exit, voice, or loyalty.[73] One can get out, speak up, or go along. Exit is the easiest, and can take the form of withdrawal from the group or, where that is impossible, "inner immigration" into alienation or passivity. Those with low levels of loyalty are likely to turn to exit. The harder choices are between voice and conformism for those with high levels of loyalty. The reason people follow a leader can be simplified into needs related to solving problems (which tend to be transactional) and needs related to identity and meaning that leaders provide (which tend to be inspirational but can also come from success in solving major problems). Problem-focused followers with a high degree of loyalty to the leader are more likely to choose voice over exit in an effort to get the leader back on the right track. Those who look to a leader to provide identity or an ideal may choose exit over voice when they lose trust and feel the leader has deceived them and is transmitting values they do not accept.[74]

More concretely, followers and leaders in the middle have a range of options when their duties to the group or organization conflict with their personal sense of integrity. Resignation is the most dramatic form of exit, but even resignation can be combined with degrees of voice and loyalty. People can resign quietly or with a public proclamation. For example, many people fault Robert McNamara for leaving quietly from his position as secretary of defense after he lost faith in the Vietnam War. They argue that he should have combined exit with voice and that a public proclamation could have shortened the war and saved lives. McNamara's response was that he was not elected and had no right to undercut a democratically elected president. After he expressed his views privately to President Johnson, he felt his obligation was to combine exit with loyalty.[75] On the other hand, in 1979, when Secretary of State Cyrus Vance disagreed with

President Carter's plan to try to rescue hostages in Iran, he told the president he would resign whatever the outcome of the action, but held his decision private until after the action so as not to prejudice its outcome. In 1973, when Attorney General Elliot Richardson and Deputy Attorney General William Ruckelshaus resigned in protest over President Nixon's firing of a special prosecutor, they publicly stated their case and had a significant effect on subsequent events.

The penalty for combining voice with exit is greater in American than in British political culture, where Parliament provides an institutional base for resignation in protest.[76] Few American politicians who resign in protest return to high office, but in Britain, nearly half do. In recent years, Robin Cook and other ministers resigned their cabinet positions quite publicly over Blair's decision to join in the invasion of Iraq. Some people have argued that Secretary of State Colin Powell should have resigned to deter President Bush from the invasion of Iraq, but Powell saw his duties to be those of internal voice and loyalty. In that choice, he fit within the dominant American political culture.

Resignation is not the only option. Followers and leaders from the middle can take a number of actions short of resignation when they find themselves unable to follow a leader's policies. Voicing internal objections may or may not be costly for one's future career, but there are times when personal integrity makes it imperative to take the risk and bear the possible cost. Leaking classified information is a more morally ambiguous way to derail a policy. It raises the difficult question of when unelected officials are justified in derailing policies for which democratically elected leaders are responsible to the electorate. Moreover, because the leaker is not likely to be caught, leaking is a tempting ploy but a deceptive one, since the leaker is not willing to pay the moral cost. At some point, personal integrity (and not just bureaucratic

gamesmanship) may justify a leak, but because of the unwillingness to pay the costs, this most prevalent of tactics is not as moral as
whistle-blowing.[77] Whistle-blowers combine voice and loyalty
in a different way. They show loyalty to their institution and to a
democratic public by publicly exposing internal wrongs and by
being willing to accept certain risks to their careers. The public
value of their actions is noted in various rules and laws designed to
protect whistle-blowers. Silence is natural. Studies show that the
exercise of critical voice is not easy in institutions. Leaders must
design learning organizations by developing the social capital of
trust, encouragement of upward communication, and systems that
operate outside the traditional hierarchy.[78]

Empowered followers (as identified in Table 5.2) also take
positive actions as well as making efforts to correct leaders when
they are headed down the wrong track. A passive or alienated
middle-level leader contributes little to the achievement of group
tasks, and conformists also do not add much value. Top leaders
cannot initiate or monitor everything in large organizations or
polities. They have only twenty-four hours in their day, and they
cannot pay attention to the myriad details that go into implementation of the visions they propound. They rely on initiative
from below to fill in the details.

Very often leaders in the middle find themselves in a policy
vacuum with few clear directives from the top. A passive follower
keeps his or her head down, shuns risk, and avoids criticism. An
opportunist uses the slack to feather his or her own nest rather
than help the leader or the public. Bureaucratic entrepreneurs, on
the other hand, take advantage of such opportunities to adjust and
promote policies. In the words of a bureaucratic veteran of the
Defense and State Departments, "Always take 20 percent more
authority than is granted. It's much better to have someone dial
you back than have to dial you forward."[79] The key moral

question is: When does such entrepreneurial activity exceed the bounds of general high-level policies set from the top? Since leaders in the middle lack the legitimate authority of elected or high-level appointed officials, they must remain cognizant of the need to balance initiative with loyalty.[80]

Leaders want to encourage such entrepreneurship among their followers as a means of increasing their effectiveness. As a popular saying goes, the key to success in leadership is to surround yourself with good people, enable them by delegation, and then claim credit for their accomplishments. To make this formula work, however, requires a good deal of soft power. Without the soft power that produces attraction and loyalty to the leader's goals, entrepreneurs run off in all directions and dissipate a group's energies. With soft power, however, the energy of empowered followers strengthens leaders.

CHOICE OF MEANS AND THE ROLE OF SOFT POWER

I began this book with the contrasting leadership views of Lao Tzu and Machiavelli and noted that the new conventional wisdom in leadership studies argues that soft power is increasingly more effective in modern democratic societies and organizations. One of the important characteristics of liberal democratic societies is that they distribute platforms for leadership broadly, whereas authoritarian regimes tend to concentrate them. As democracy spreads, leadership opportunities become more widespread, but leaders find it more difficult to exercise hard power. Soft power skills of attraction and persuasion become more important. Leaders have to pay more attention to how they adjust to flatter hierarchies and find ways to empower their followers. Instead of just shaping others to their will, leaders have to attract support by also shaping themselves to their followers. If having hard power traditionally meant enjoying the privilege of not having to adjust or learn, wielding soft power often requires learning and adapting to followers' needs.[81] At the same time, however, I noted that hard power remains an essential tool for effective leaders even in modern democratic societies. Contextual intelligence is necessary if leaders wish to understand the appropriate mix of hard and soft power skills in particular situations.

Turning from the effective to the ethical dimension, are there moral grounds to prefer soft power? Not always. During the American Civil War, General George McClellan was popular and attracted the loyalty of his troops (and many in Congress) but was feckless in his use of hard power as a general. Moreover, as we saw earlier, soft power is not good per se. In terms of leaders' goals, soft power can be used for good or nefarious purposes, and it can produce good or bad consequences. If someone steals your wealth by soft power, the consequence is still theft. To take a more dramatic example, Osama bin Laden used his soft power to attract nineteen people to commit suicide and mass murder on September 11, 2001. But on the dimension of means, as opposed to goals and consequences, I argued that a moral case can be made for preferring soft power. By its very nature, it depends on what goes on in the mind of the followers and usually leaves more space for others to exercise choice. If we value autonomy of individuals and respect their choices, then, although coercion may sometimes be necessary, it should be generally disfavored, and it is usually more moral for a leader who has options to prefer soft power.

Coercion is a matter of degree. The economic part of hard power rests on inducements that may not seem coercive. But as we saw earlier, a leader can always take away a reward and turn an inducement into a threat. Some inducements (and the threat of their removal) may be more enabling and others more coercive in the eyes of followers.

Skeptics argue that soft power is coercive as well. In a broad sense in which coercion implies any pressure to compel behavior, words can be coercive, and twisting minds can feel manipulative. In a war of words, competitive attractions certainly feel coercive. If some modern Pied Piper threatens to lure your child away from you, or a competitor runs advertisements designed to deprive you of your supporters, such verbal and nonmaterial threats may seem very coercive. At the same time, there is still some wisdom in the old adage that sticks and stones can break your bones, but words don't really hurt you. Of course words can hurt, but you have more options in response to words than to force (which may be why the dictionary also includes a second definition of coercion as control by force). Soft power may feel threatening and manipulative, but it still leaves open a wider range of choices in the target's response.[82]

Soft power instruments are not all equal in this regard. They differ in the degree of rational appeal and respect for followers' autonomy. Leaders can create or destroy institutions that protect such distinctions. Educating the public is not the same as indoctrinating the public with propaganda. There is an important difference of degree between Roosevelt's fireside radio broadcasts and Hitler's elaborately staged Nuremberg rallies. Persuasion has different degrees of emotional appeal, and an excessive rhetoric of group cohesion, patriotism, and collective identity is designed to drive out reason and limit individual autonomy. Propaganda and ideology that approach brainwashing may so program followers that they are not even aware of the manipulation. In such cases, soft power instruments can create a psychological manipulation that provides as little choice as hard power, but these circumstances often depend on a coercive order that limits access to alternative views. When these circumstances are absent, however, a preference for soft means can be morally justified.

Some soft power means are better than others. Rhetoric and argument may slip into brainwashing, but Lao Tzu's quiet approach and leadership by example are less susceptible to this type of manipulation. Gandhi's salt march, King's nonviolent resistance, and Mandela's embrace of a broad South African identity left multiple options open for followers. But contrary to the nearly invisible leadership preached by the Asian philosopher, each of these great soft power leaders also relied on the visibility of their charisma to move their followers. As we saw earlier, charisma itself raises interesting moral issues as a soft power instrument. When combined with narcissism, it can be highly dangerous. When wielded by balanced leaders, personal attraction can mobilize people for new goals and objectives, but a danger arises when leaders use the soft power of their charisma to weaken institutional constraints that maintain the potential for alternative Madisonian solutions to group problems.

Power is the ability to affect others to obtain the outcomes one wants, but we can also distinguish between simply wanting power *over* others and wanting power *with* others. Getting what you want and enabling others to do what they want can be reconciled or linked by soft power skills of listening, mutual persuasion, communicating, and education. Power in a relationship need not be a zero-sum situation, and, as described earlier, empowering followers can better enable a leader to achieve his or her desired outcomes. This may be the central message of Lao Tzu's ancient insight that "a leader is best when people barely know he exists, not so good when people obey and acclaim him; worst when they despise him."[83] In today's world, the leader will need to combine various soft power skills with Machiavellian hard power skills, but a

moral case can be made that leaders should have a general preference for soft power options when possible. Fortunately, if the new
conventional wisdom about democratization and the information
age is correct that followers have more power than ever before,
leaders may find that what is ethical and what is effective may
coincide more often than in the past.

We judge our leaders every day. Sometimes the categories and
judgments are easy, as in the cases described at the beginning of
this chapter. At other times, there are subtle trade-offs among
ends, means, and consequences. In balancing moral obligations
suggested by their conscience, common moral rules, and their
fiduciary roles, leaders sometimes have to accept the burden of
dirty hands because of their roles. But difficult dilemmas should
invite rather than discourage moral discourse. Societies, groups,
and leaders are all better off for engaging in open practices of
criticism that use the distinctions suggested earlier.

The good news is that leaders can change. They are mostly
made, not born, and leadership can be learned. McClelland and
Burnham, whose work on power was cited at the beginning of this
chapter, found that managers can be trained to change their style.
They suggest that the best leaders "possess two characteristics that
act as regulators—a greater emotional maturity, where there is
little egotism, and a democratic, coaching managerial style."[84] As
we saw earlier, emotional maturity, self-awareness, and emotional
intelligence can also be learned and taught.[85] Both individuals and
organizations can learn.[86]

Leadership is not learned primarily from books, but a book like
this can help make people more aware of the lessons of history and
psychology so they can recognize and better understand the skills
they need. Art history does not produce great painters, but it can
help develop and educate intuitions. Leadership is broadly distributed throughout healthy democracies, and all citizens need to

learn more about what makes good and bad leaders. Potential leaders, in turn, can learn more about the sources and limits of the soft power skills of emotional IQ, vision, and communication as well as hard power political and organizational skills. They must also better understand the nature of the contextual intelligence they will need to educate their hunches and sustain strategies of smart power. Most important, in today's age of globalization, information revolution, and broadened participation, citizens in democracies must learn more about the nature and limits of our all-too-human leadership.

Leadership: A Dozen Quick Take-Aways

1. Good leadership matters. *Good = effective and ethical.* Luck matters for success, but good leaders can help shape their luck.
2. Almost anyone can become a leader. *Leadership can be learned.* It depends on nurture as well as on nature. Leadership can exist at any level, with or without formal authority. Most people are both leaders and followers. They "lead from the middle."
3. Leaders help *create and achieve group goals.* Thus effectiveness requires *both* vision *and* interpersonal/organizational skills.
4. Smart leaders need both *soft and hard power skills*: co-optive and command styles. Both *transformational and transactional* objectives and styles can be useful. One is not automatically better than the other.
5. Leaders depend on and are *partly shaped by followers.* Some degree of soft power is necessary. Presence/magnetism is inherent in some personalities more than others, but *"charisma"* is largely bestowed by followers.
6. *Appropriate style depends on the context.* There are "autocratic situations" and "democratic situations," normal and crisis conditions, and routine and novel crises. Good diagnosis of the need for change (or not) is essential for *contextual intelligence.*

7. A *consultative style* is more costly in terms of time, but it *provides more information, creates buy-in, and empowers followers.*

8. Managers are not necessarily leaders, but effective leaders usually need *both managerial and organizational skills.* They create and maintain systems and institutions. Leaders are not mere deciders; they help a group decide how to decide.

9. Leadership for *crisis* conditions requires advanced preparation, emotional maturity, and the ability to distinguish the roles of *operational, analytical, and political work.* The appropriate mix of styles and skills varies with the stage of the crisis. Experience creates tacit knowledge, but *analysis* also counts. A cat that sits on a hot stove will not sit there again, but it will not sit on a cold stove either.

10. The information revolution and democratization are causing a long-term *secular shift in the context of postmodern organizations*—a shift along the continuum from command to co-optive style. Network organizations require a more consultative style. While sometimes stereotyped as a feminine style, both men and women face this change and need to adapt to it. *Empowered followers empower leaders.*

11. Reality testing, constant information seeking, and adjusting to change are essential for good consequences, but *emotional intelligence* and *practical knowledge* are more important than pure IQ in judgment.

12. Ethical leaders use their consciences, common moral rules, and professional standards, but conflicting values can create "*dirty hands.*" Three-dimensional ethical judgments require attention to *goals, means, and consequences* for those inside and outside the leader's group. Creating identities in intergroup leadership is difficult but crucial.

Notes

Preface

1. Lao Tzu, *Tao Te Ching: A New English Version*, with foreword and notes by Stephen Mitchell (London: Macmillan, 1988), 19.
2. Niccolò Machiavelli, *The Prince* (New York: New American Library Mentor Book, 1952), chapter 17.
3. Silla Brush, "A Vote of No Confidence," *U.S. News & World Report*, October 30, 2006, p. 56. See also *National Leadership Index 2006: A National Study of Confidence in Leadership* (http://www.ksg.harvard.edu/nli).
4. For a discussion of causes, see Joseph S. Nye Jr., Philip Zelikow, and David King, eds., *Why People Don't Trust Government* (Cambridge, MA: Harvard University Press, 1997).
5. Bill George (the former CEO of Medtronics), "Truly Authentic Leadership," *U.S. News & World Report*, October 30, 2006, p. 52.
6. Robert C. Tucker contrasts a power approach with a leadership approach in *Politics as Leadership*, rev. ed. (Columbia: University of Missouri Press, 1995), chapter 1.
7. Quoted in David S. Cloud, "Here's Donny! In His Defense, a Show Is Born," *New York Times*, April 19, 2006, pp. A1, A15.
8. Joseph Rost, quoted in Joanne B. Ciulla, *The Ethics of Leadership* (Belmont, CA: Thompson Wadsworth, 2003), xii.
9. Joseph C. Rost, *Leadership for the Twenty-First Century* (Westport, CT: Praeger, 1991), 7.

10. Michelle C. Bligh and James R. Meindl, "The Cultural Ecology of Leadership: An Analysis of Popular Leadership Books," in David M. Messick and Roderick M. Kramer, eds., *The Psychology of Leadership: New Perspectives and Research* (Mahwah, NJ: Lawrence Erlbaum, 2005), 11–52, 32.

Chapter 1

1. Eric Schmidt, Bernhard Schwartz Lecture on Business and Foreign Policy at the Council on Foreign Relations, New York, June 8, 2006; Daniel Nye, CEO of LinkedIn, personal correspondence, May 2007.

2. Undersecretary of Defense David S. Chu and Lt. Col. Mike Jones, head of Army National Guard recruiting, quoted in Associated Press, "Pentagon Softens Instructor's Role," *Washington Times*, October 11, 2006, p. 4.

3. Victor H. Vroom, "Leadership and Decision Making Processes," *Organizational Dynamics* 28, no. 4 (2000): 92.

4. Roderick M. Kramer, "The Great Intimidators," *Harvard Business Review* 84, no. 2 (2006): 88–96.

5. Warren G. Bennis, "Where Have All the Leaders Gone?" *Technology Review* 79 (1977): 3–12.

6. See Scott T. Allison and Dafna Eylon, "The Demise of Leadership: Death Positivity Biases in Posthumous Impressions of Leaders," in David M. Messick and Roderick M. Kramer, eds., *The Psychology of Leadership: New Perspectives and Research* (Mahwah, NJ: Lawrence Erlbaum, 2005), 295–317.

7. Henry Mintzberg, "Community-Ship Is the Answer," *Financial Times*, October 23, 2006, p. 8.

8. J. Richard Hackman, *Leading Teams: Setting the Stage for Great Performance* (Boston: Harvard Business School Press, 2002), 199–200, 204, 211–12.

9. Stanley Lieberson and James F. O'Connor, "Leadership and Organizational Performance: A Study of Large Corporations," *American Sociological Review* 37, no. 2 (1972): 118.

10. James R. Meindl, Sanford B. Ehrlich, and Janet M. Dukeich, "The Romance of Leadership," *Administrative Science Quarterly* 30 (1985): 79–80.

11. Boris Groysberg, Andrew N. McLean, and Nitin Nohria, "Are Leaders Portable?" *Harvard Business Review* 84, no. 5 (2006): 95.

12. Noam Wasserman, Bharat Anand, and Nitin Nohria, "When Does Leadership Matter? The Contingent Opportunities View of CEO Leadership," *Working Paper 01–063*, Harvard Business School, Cambridge, MA, April 2001. See also Lieberson and O'Connor, "Leadership and Organizational Performance"; and Alan Berkeley Thomas, "Does Leadership Make a Difference to Organizational Performance?" *Administrative Science Quarterly* 33, no. 3 (1988): 388–400.

13. Michael D. Cohen and James G. March, *Leadership and Ambiguity: The American College President* (Boston: Harvard Business School Press, 1986); Jeffrey Pfeffer and Gerald Salancik, *The External Control of Organizations: A Resource Dependence Perspective* (New York: Harper & Row, 1978); Jeffrey Pfeffer, "The Ambiguity of Leadership," *The Academy of Management Review* 2, no. 1 (1977): 104–12.

14. J. Richard Hackman and Ruth Wageman, "When and How Team Leaders Matter," *Research in Organizational Behavior* 26 (2005): 64.

15. Thomas Carlyle, "The Leader as Hero," and Herbert Spencer, "The Great Man Theory Breaks Down," in Barbara Kellerman, ed., *Political Leadership: A Source Book* (Pittsburgh, PA: University of Pittsburgh Press, 1986), 5, 13, respectively.

16. Karl Marx, *The Eighteenth Brumaire of Louis Bonaparte* (New York: International Publishers, 1963), 15.

17. Quoted in Edward Rothstein, "Churchill, Heroic Relic or Relevant Now?" *New York Times*, March 29, 2003, pp. D7.

18. Sidney Hook, "The Eventful Man and the Event-Making Man," in Kellerman, *Political Leadership*, 25–27.

19. Philip Stephens, "Ten Years on, a New Set of Rules," *Financial Times*, May 1, 2007, p. 13.

20. Of course, not every individual who creates a fork in the road of history is a leader—witness Lee Harvey Oswald's assassination of John F. Kennedy.

21. David Gelernter, *Americanism: The Fourth Great Western Religion* (New York: Doubleday, 2007), 199.

22. In a curious footnote to this history, when I asked him at his seventy-fifth birthday celebration in Moscow in 2005 how he

looked back on his actions, Gorbachev replied, "I have no regrets. I wish I had done more."

23. Clifford Bob and Sharon Erickson Nepstad, "Kill a Leader, Murder a Movement? Leadership and Assassination in Social Movements," *American Behavioral Scientist* 50, no. 10 (2007): 1370–94.

24. See Robert C. Tucker, *Politics as Leadership*, rev. ed. (Columbia: University of Missouri Press, 1995), 30.

25. Henry Kissinger, *Diplomacy* (New York: Simon & Schuster, 1994).

26. John W. Kingdon, *Agendas, Alternatives, and Public Policies*, 2nd ed. (New York: Longman, 2003), 224–26.

27. Thomas Carlyle, *On Heroes, Hero Worship, and the Heroic in History* (New York: Ginn, 1902), 226.

28. Peter H. Gibbon, *A Call to Heroism: Renewing America's Vision to Greatness* (New York: Atlantic Monthly Press, 2002).

29. Arnold M. Ludwig, *King of the Mountain: The Nature of Political Leadership* (Lexington: University Press of Kentucky, 2002), 293.

30. Robert D. Kaplan, *Warrior Politics: Why Leadership Demands a Pagan Ethos* (New York: Random House, 2002), 119.

31. General James Thurman, quoted in Anna Mulrine, "Emphasizing Ethics Even as Bullets Fly," *U.S. News & World Report*, June 19, 2006, 25.

32. Paul S. Oh and David E. Lewis, "Management and Leadership Performance in the Defense Department: Evidence from Surveys of Federal Employees," *Armed Forces and Society*, forthcoming.

33. Xenophon, *The Education of Cyrus*, translated by Henry Graham Dakyns (New York: E. P. Dutton, 1914), 5.

34. For an excellent portrayal of the effects, see William Taubman's *Khrushchev: The Man and His Era* (New York: Norton, 2003).

35. Women tyrants are rare in history, but perhaps that is because most women were denied the opportunity. Elizabeth I of England and Russia's Catherine the Great were not exactly gentle leaders.

36. Ludwig, *King of the Mountain*.

37. Ronald A. Heifetz, *Leadership without Easy Answers* (Cambridge, MA: Belknap Press of Harvard University Press, 1994), 49–66.

38. Samuel Johnson, quoted in Richard Wrangham and Dale Peterson, *Demonic Males: Apes and the Origins of Human Violence* (New York: Houghton Mifflin, 1996), 191.

39. Richard D. Arvey, Maria Rotundo, Wendy Johnson, Zhen Zhang, and Matt McGue, "The Determinants of Leadership Role Occupancy: Genetic and Personality Factors," *Leadership Quarterly* 17, no. 1 (2006): 1–20.

40. Shirley C. Shrum and Linda M. Fedigan, eds., *Primate Encounters: Models of Science, Gender and Society* (Chicago: University of Chicago Press, 2000).

41. Robert M. Sapolsky, "The Influence of Social Hierarchy on Primate Health," *Science* 308, no. 5722 (2005): 648–52; and Sapolsky, "A Natural History of Peace," *Foreign Affairs* 85, no. 1 (2006): 104–20.

42. Christopher Boehm, *Hierarchy in the Forest: The Evolution of Egalitarian Behavior* (Cambridge, MA: Harvard University Press, 1999), 10.

43. Bruce M. Knauft, "Violence and Sociality in Human Evolution," *Current Anthropology* 32, no. 4 (1991): 391–428.

44. Malcolm Gladwell, *Blink: The Power of Thinking without Thinking* (New York: Little, Brown, 2005), 88.

45. Alan Bryman, "Leadership in Organizations," in Stewart Clegg, Cynthia Hardy, and Walter Nord, eds., *Handbook of Organization Studies* (London: Sage, 1996), 277. See also R. M. Stogdill, "Personal Factors Associated with Leadership: A Survey of the Literature," *Journal of Psychology* 25 (1948): 35–71.

46. Stephen J. Zaccaro, "Trait-Based Perspectives of Leadership," *American Psychologist* 62, no. 1 (2007): 7.

47. Markus M. Mobius and Tanja S. Rosenblat, "Why Beauty Matters," *American Economic Review* 96, no. 1 (2006): 222–35.

48. Mark Allen argues this in *Arabs* (New York: Continuum, 2006).

49. John H. Clippinger, *A Crowd of One: The Future of Individual Identity* (New York: Public Affairs, 2007), 88.

50. Walter Isaacson, *Einstein: His Life and Universe* (New York: Simon & Schuster, 2007). I am indebted to Isaacson for a discussion of Einstein and leadership.

51. Quoted in Lee Smolin, "The Other Einstein," *The New York Review of Books*, June 14, 2007, p. 81.

52. Garry Wills, *Certain Trumpets: The Call of Leaders* (New York: Simon & Schuster, 1994), 16.

53. Doris Kearns Goodwin, *Team of Rivals: The Political Genius of Abraham Lincoln* (New York: Simon & Schuster, 2005).

54. Wills, *Certain Trumpets*, 16.

55. Douglas Brinkley, *Rosa Parks* (New York: Penguin Viking Lipper, 2000), 103–18.

56. Jo Reger, "Introduction: New Dimensions in the Study of Social Movement Leadership," *American Behavioral Scientist* 50, no. 10 (2007): 1304.

57. On leading with and without authority, see Ronald A. Heifetz, "Leadership, Authority, and Women," in Barbara Kellerman and Deborah L. Rhode, eds., *Women and Leadership* (San Francisco: Wiley, 2007), 314–21; and Heifetz, *Leadership without Easy Answers* (Cambridge, MA: Belknap Press of Harvard University Press, 1994).

58. Barbara Kellerman, *Bad Leadership: What It Is, How It Happens, Why It Matters* (Boston: Harvard Business School Press, 2004), 21–25.

59. Hackman, *Leading Teams*, 211.

60. J. Richard Hackman, "Rethinking Team Leadership or Team Leaders Are Not Music Directors," in David M. Messick and Roderick M. Kramer, eds., *The Psychology of Leadership: New Persepctives and Research* (Mahwah, NJ: Lawrence Erlbaum, 2005), 119; E. V. Lehmann and J. Richard Hackman, "Nobody on the Podium: Lessons for Leaders from the Orpheus Chamber Orchestra," *Case No. 1644.9,* John F. Kennedy School of Government, Harvard University, Cambridge, MA, 2002; Sidney Harman, *Mind Your Own Business* (New York: Currency/Doubleday, 2003), 6.

61. James O'Toole, Jay Galbraith, and Edward E. Lawler III, "The Promise and Pitfalls of Shared Leadership: When Two (or More) Heads Are Better Than One," and Edwin Locke, "Leadership Starting at the Top," in Craig L. Pearce and Jay A. Conger, eds., *Shared Leadership: Reframing the Hows and Whys of Leadership* (Thousand Oaks, CA: Sage, 2003), 250–68 and 269–84, respectively; David A. Heenan and Warren G. Bennis, *Co-Leaders: The Power of Great Partnerships* (New York: Wiley, 1999).

62. Jay A. Conger and Craig L. Pearce, "A Landscape of Opportunities: Future Research on Shared Leadership," in Pearce and Conger, *Shared Leadership*, 289.

63. Some experts go so far as to define leadership simply as "the process of being perceived by others as a leader." Robert Lord and Karen Maher, *Leadership and Information Processing: Linking Perceptions and Performance* (Boston: Unwin Hyman, 1991), 11.

64. See Jonathan Purkis, "Leaderless Cultures: The Problem of Authority in a Radical Environmental Group," in Colin Barker, Alan Johnson, and Michael Lavalette, eds., *Leadership and Social Movements* (Manchester, UK: Manchester University Press, 2001), 160–77.

65. Hackman and Wageman, "When and How Team Leaders Matter," 43. For a useful survey of the changing definitions of leadership over the decades, see Joanne B. Ciulla, "Leadership Ethics: Mapping the Territory," in Joanne B. Ciulla, *Ethics: The Heart of Leadership*, 2nd ed. (Westport, CT: Praeger, 2004), 10; see also Joseph C. Rost, *Leadership for the Twenty-First Century* (Westport, CT: Praeger, 1991), chapters 3 and 4.

66. Bill George, Peter Sims, Andrew N. McLean, and Diana Mayer, "Discovering Your Authentic Leadership," *Harvard Business Review* 85, no. 2 (2007): 129.

67. Keith Grint, *The Arts of Leadership* (Oxford: Oxford University Press, 2000), 3.

68. Alan Bryman, "Leadership in Organizations," in Stewart R. Clegg, Cynthia Hardy, and Walter R. Nord, eds., *Handbook of Organization Studies* (London: Sage, 1996), 276–92.

69. Grint, *The Arts of Leadership*, 4.

70. Hackman, *Leading Teams*, 216.

71. Alan Schussman and Jennifer Earl, "From Barricades to Firewalls? Strategic Voting and Social Movement Leadership in the Internet Age," *Sociological Inquiry* 74, no. 4 (2004): 459.

72. Keith Grint, *Leadership: Classical, Contemporary, and Critical Approaches* (Oxford: Oxford University Press, 1997), 2.

73. Frances Hesselbein and General Eric K. Shinseki, *Be-Know-Do: Leadership the Army Way: Adapted from the Official Army Leadership*

Manual (San Francisco: Jossey-Bass, 2004). See also Scott Snook and Rakesh Khurana, "Developing 'Leaders of Character': Lessons from West Point," Harvard Business School, unpublished manuscript.

74. Sharon Daloz Parks, *Leadership Can Be Taught: A Bold Approach for a Complex World* (Boston: Harvard Business School Press, 2005).

Chapter 2

1. For a classic exploration of this problem, see James G. March, "The Power of Power," in David Easton, ed., *Varieties of Political Theory* (Englewood Cliffs, NJ: Prentice-Hall, 1966), 39–70. See also Steven Lukes, *Power: A Radical View*, 2nd ed. (London: Palgrave, 2005). Classic articles on power by Robert Dahl, John C. Harsanyi, Hebert Simon, and others are collected in Roderick Bell, David V. Edwards, and R. Harrison Wagner, eds., *Political Power: A Reader in Theory and Research* (New York: Free Press, 1969).

2. In *Power: A Radical View*, Steven Lukes even *defines* power as the ability to make, receive, and resist change.

3. Adam Galinsky, Joe C. Magee, M. Ena Inesi, and Deborah Gruenfeld, "Power and Perspectives Not Taken," *Psychological Science* 17, no. 12 (2006): 1068–74.

4. Robert A. Dahl, *Who Governs? Democracy and Power in an American City* (New Haven, CT: Yale University Press, 1961).

5. David Baldwin, "Power Analysis and World Politics: New Trends versus Old Tendencies," *World Politics* 31, no. 2 (1979): 161–94.

6. I first introduced this concept in Joseph S. Nye Jr., *Bound to Lead: The Changing Nature of American Power* (New York: Basic Books, 1990), chapter 2. It builds on but differs from what Peter Bachrach and Morton Baratz called the "second face of power." See Peter Bachrach and Morton S. Baratz, "Decisions and Nondecisions: An Analytical Framework," *American Political Science Review* 57, no. 3 (1963): 632–42.

7. Karen Christensen, "Putting Power into Practice: An Interview with Rosabeth Moss Kanter," *Rotman Magazine*, Spring/Summer 2005, 17.

8. Thom Shanker, "Retiring Army Chief of Staff Warns against Arrogance," *New York Times*, June 12, 2003, p. A32.

9. A well-known taxonomy of power resources differentiates five types of power: coercive, reward, legitimate, referent, and expert. The first two fall into my hard power category, the other three into soft power. See John R. P. French and Bertram H. Raven, "The Bases of Social Power," in Dorwin Cartwright, ed., *Studies in Social Power* (Ann Arbor, MI: Institute of Social Research, 1959), 150–67. Gary A. Yukl and Cecilia. M. Falbe, "The Importance of Different Power Sources in Downward and Lateral Relations," *Journal of Applied Psychology* 76 (1991): 416–23, add persuasiveness and control of information, which I include as soft power resources.

10. The word "influence" is used in various ways. I treat it as synonymous with behavioral power, which is consistent with the dictionary.

11. See Jane J. Mansbridge, *Beyond Self-Interest* (Chicago: University of Chicago Press, 1990).

12. I am endebted to Mark Moore for this point and other discussions.

13. Richard Neustadt, *Presidential Power and the Modern Presidents: The Politics of Leadership from Rosevelt to Reagan* (New York: Free Press, 1990), 11.

14. Quoted in Alan Axelrod, *Eisenhower on Leadership: Ike's Enduring Lessons in Total Victory Management* (San Francisco: Jossey-Bass, 2006), 120, 283.

15. Charles Lindholm, *Charisma* (Cambridge, MA: Blackwell, 1990), chapter 10.

16. The 2006 German film *Downfall* depicts this episode brilliantly as an example of Hitler's soft power.

17. Christopher Hodgkinson, *The Philosophy of Leadership* (New York: St. Martin's Press, 1983), 163.

18. Keith Grint, *The Arts of Leadership* (Oxford: Oxford University Press, 2000), 332.

19. Barbara Kellerman, *Followership: How Followers Are Creating Change and Changing Leaders* (Boston: Harvard Business School Press, forthcoming).

20. James C. Scott, *Domination and the Arts of Resistance: Hidden Transcripts* (New Haven, CT: Yale University Press, 1990).

21. Ronald A. Heifetz, *Leadership without Easy Answers* (Cambridge, MA: Belknap Press of Harvard University Press, 1994).

22. Kellerman, *Followership*; see also Robert E. Kelley, *The Power of Followership: How to Create Leaders People Want to Follow, and Followers Who Lead Themselves* (New York: Doubleday/Currency, 1992).

23. Richard N. Haass, *The Bureaucratic Entrepreneur: How to Be Effective in Any Unruly Organization* (Washington, DC: Brookings Institution Press, 1999), 2.

24. Robert G. Lord and Karen J. Maher, *Leadership and Information Processing: Linking Perceptions and Performance* (Boston: Unwin Hyman, 1991), 59.

25. Comte de Mirabeau, quoted in Hodgkinson, *The Philosophy of Leadership*, 163.

26. James MacGregor Burns and Susan Dunn, *The Three Roosevelts: Patrician Leaders Who Transformed America* (New York: Grove Press, 2002).

27. Christopher Boehm, *Hierarchy in the Forest: The Evolution of Egalitarian Behavior* (Cambridge, MA: Harvard University Press, 1999).

28. Siobhan O'Mahony, "Governance in Production Communities," unpublished manuscript, 2007.

29. George Edwards, *On Deaf Ears: The Limits of the Bully Pulpit* (New Haven, CT: Yale University Press, 2003), 119.

30. Lukes, *Power*, 11.

31. Max Weber, "Types of Authority," in Barbara Kellerman, ed., *Political Leadership: A Source Book* (Pittsburgh, PA: University of Pittsburgh Press, 1986), 232–44.

32. Gary A. Yukl and David D. Van Fleet, "Theory and Research on Leadership in Organizations," in Marvin D. Dunnette and Leaetta M. Hough, eds., *Handbook of Industrial and Organizational Psychology*, 2nd ed. (Palo Alto, CA: Consulting Psychologists Press, 1992), 3: 147–97.

33. See Colin Barker, Alan Johnson, and Michael Lavalette, eds., *Leadership and Social Movements* (Manchester, UK: Manchester University Press, 2001).

34. Ronald A. Heifetz, "The Scholarly/Practical Challenge of Leadership," in Richard A. Couto, ed., *Reflections on Leadership* (Lanham, MD: University Press of America, 2007), 32.

35. Sheryl Gay Stolberg, "For President Bush, a Reversal of Fortune on His Political Control," *New York Times*, June 30, 2007, p. A11.

36. Lukes, *Power*. See also Janice Bially Mattern, "Why Soft Power Isn't So Soft: Representational Force and the Sociolinguistic Construction of Attraction in World Politics," *Millennium* 33, no. 3 (2005): 583–612.

37. Ruth W. Grant, "Ethics and Incentives: A Political Approach," *American Political Science Review* 100, no. 1 (2006): 32. Grant distinguishes three forms of power: force, exchange, and speech. My third category of attraction is broader by including charisma and example as well as persuasive speech.

38. Robert O. Keohane and Joseph S. Nye, *Power and Interdependence* (Boston: Little, Brown, 1977).

39. Adam Smith, *The Theory of Moral Sentiments* (New York: A. M. Kelley, 1966), 84.

40. Quoted in "A Nation Challenged; Scenes of Rejoicing and Words of Strategy from bin Laden and His Allies," *New York Times*, December 14, 2001, p. B4.

41. Richard S. Tedlow, "What Titans Can Teach Us," *Harvard Business Review* 79, no. 11 (2001): 74.

42. Roderick M. Kramer, "The Great Intimidators," *Harvard Business Review* 84, no. 2 (2006): 95.

43. Jameson W. Doig and Erwin C. Hargrove, eds., *Leadership and Innovation: Entrepreneurs in Government* (Baltimore: Johns Hopkins University Press, 1990).

44. Michael G. Harvey, Joyce T. Heames, R. Glenn Richey, and Nancy Leonard, "Bullying: From the Playground to the Boardroom," *Journal of Leadership and Organizational Studies* 12, no. 4 (2006): 1–11.

45. Chris Patten, *Cousins and Strangers: America, Britain, and Europe in a New Century*, 1st American ed. (New York: Times Books, 2006), 119.

46. Katrina Bedell, Samuel Hunter, Amanda Angie, and Andrew Vert, "A Historiometric Examination of Machiavellianism and a New Taxonomy of Leadership," *Journal of Leadership and Organizational Studies*

12, no. 4 (2006): 50–72. But see Ronald J. Deluga, "American Presidential Machiavellianism: Implications for Charismatic Leadership and Rated Performance," *Leadership Quarterly* 12, no. 3 (2001): 339–63, and Dean K. Simonton, "Presidential Personality: Biographical Use of the Gough Adjective Check List," *Journal of Personality and Social Psychology* 51, no. 1 (1986): 149–60, for opposing findings.

47. Mark Mazzetti, "Spy Agencies Say Iraq War Worsens Terrorism Threat," *New York Times*, September 24, 2006, p. 1.

48. James MacGregor Burns, *Leadership* (New York: Harper & Row, 1978), 3.

49. David Hume, "Of the First Principles of Government," in *Essays Moral, Political and Literary*, edited by Eugene F. Miller (Indianapolis, IN: Liberty Classics, 1985), 32–33.

50. Daniel R. Ames and Francis J. Flynn, "What Breaks a Leader: The Curvilinear Relation between Assertiveness and Leadership," *Journal of Personality and Social Psychology* 92, no. 2 (2007): 308.

51. Quoted in Joe Nocera, "Running GE, Comfortable in His Skin," *New York Times*, June 9, 2007, p. C9.

52. Niccolò Machiavelli, *The Prince* (New York: New American Library, 1952), chapter 17.

53. Thomas L. Friedman, *The World Is Flat: A Brief History of the Twenty-First Century* (New York: Farrar, Straus and Giroux, 2006); Frances Cairncross, *The Death of Distance: How the Communications Revolution Will Change Our Lives* (Boston: Harvard Business School Press, 2001).

54. Ronald S. Burt, *Structural Holes: The Social Structure of Competition* (Cambridge, MA: Harvard University Press, 1992).

55. Hubs can generate data, organize the data into information, and analyze that information to create knowledge. Some hubs are better designed than others to organize and analyze information into knowledge, and thus more important to leaders from a power perspective. I am indebted to Dutch Leonard for this point.

56. Mark Granovetter, "The Myth of Social Network Analysis as a Special Method in the Social Sciences," *Connections* 13, no. 2 (1990): 13–16.

57. Daniel J. Brass and David Krackhardt, "The Social Capital of Twenty-First Century Leaders," in James G. Hunt, George E. Dodge, and Leonard Wong, eds., *Out-of-the-Box Leadership Challenges for the 21st Century Army and Other Top-Performing Organizations* (Stamford, CT: JAI Press, 1999), 191.

58. Justine Cassell, David Huffaker, Dona Tversky, and Kim Ferriman, "The Language of Online Leadership: Gender and Youth Engagement on the Internet," *Developmental Psychology* 42, no. 3 (2006): 436–49.

59. Benedict Anderson, *Imagined Communities: Reflections on the Origin and Spread of Nationalism*, rev. ed. (New York: Verso, 1991).

60. Frances Hesselbein and Marshall Goldsmith, eds., *The Leader of the Future 2: Visions, Strategies, and Practices for the New Era* (San Francisco: Jossey-Bass, 2006); Todd L. Pittinsky, R. Matthew Montoya, and Linda R. Tropp, "Leader Influences on Positive and Negative Intergroup Emotions," paper presented at the 10th annual meeting of Research on Managing Groups and Teams, Cornell and Stanford Universities, May 2006.

61. Todd L. Pittinsky and Margaret J. Shih, "Leading the Knowledge Nomad," in Robert Gandossy, Nidhi Verma, and Elissa Tucker, eds., *Workforce Wake-up Call: Your Workforce Is Changing, Are You?* (Hoboken, NJ: Wiley, 2006), 95–100; Elaine C. Kamarck, The *End of Government . . . as We Know It: Making Public Policy Work* (Boulder, CO: Lynne Rienner Publishers, 2007).

62. John Gapper, "Companies Feel Benefit of Intangibles," *Financial Times Special Report on Global Brands*, April 23, 2007, p. 1.

63. Philip Evans and Bob Wolf, "Collaboration Rules," *Harvard Business Review* 83, no. 7 (2005): 102.

64. Samuel J. Palmisano, "The Globally Integrated Enterprise," *Foreign Affairs* 85, no. 3 (2006): 134.

65. Michael E. Brown and Dennis Gioia, "Making Things Click: Distributive Leadership in an Online Division of an Offline Organization," *Leadership Quarterly* 13, no. 4 (2002): 410.

66. John Quelch, "How Soft Power Is Winning Hearts, Minds, and Influence," *Financial Times*, October 10, 2005, p. 17.

67. Jim Collins, *Good to Great: Why Some Companies Make the Leap . . . and Others Don't* (New York: Harper Business, 2001); Bill George with Peter Sims, *True North: Discover Your Authentic Leadership* (San Francisco: Wiley, 2007).

68. Victor H. Vroom, "Leadership and Decision Making Processes," *Organizational Dynamics* 28, no. 4 (2000): 82–94.

69. Joseph S. Nye Jr., Philip D. Zelikow, and David C. King, eds., *Why People Don't Trust Government* (Cambridge, MA: Harvard University Press, 1997).

70. David Osborne and Ted Gaebler, *Reinventing Government: How the Entrepreneurial Spirit Is Transforming the Public Sector* (Reading, MA: Addison-Wesley, 1992), 28.

71. I am indebted to Matt Kohut for this example.

72. Evans and Wolf, "Collaboration Rules," 102.

73. Joyce K. Fletcher, "The Paradox of Postheroic Leadership: An Essay on Gender, Power, and Transformational Change," *Leadership Quarterly* 15, no. 5 (2004): 648.

74. Judy B. Rosener, "Ways Women Lead," *Harvard Business Review* 68, no. 6 (1990): 123.

75. Alice H. Eagly and Blair T. Johnson, "Gender and Leadership Style: A Meta-Analysis," *Psychological Bulletin* 108 (1990): 233–56. See also Gary N. Powell, *Women and Men in Management*, 3rd ed. (Thousand Oaks, CA: Sage, 2003); Deborah L. Rhode, ed., *The Difference "Difference" Makes: Women and Leadership* (Stanford: Stanford University Press, 2003).

76. Arnold Ludwig, *King of the Mountain: The Nature of Political Leadership* (Lexington: University Press of Kentucky, 2002), 22–23.

77. Hannah Riley Bowles and Kathleen L. McGinn, "Claiming Authority: Negotiating Challenges for Women Leaders," in David M. Messick and Roderick M. Kramer, eds., *The Psychology of Leadership: New Perspectives and Research* (Mahwah, NJ: Lawrence Erlbaum, 2005), 192. I am indebted to Hannah Bowles for help on this section.

78. Daniel J. Brass, "Men's and Women's Networks: A Study of Interaction Patterns and Influence in an Organization," *Academy of Management Journal* 28, no. 2 (1985): 327–43; Herminia Ibarra, "Personal Networks of Women and Minorities in Management:

A Conceptual Framework," *Academy of Management Review* 18, no. 1 (1993): 56–87.

79. Marjukka Ollilainen, "Gendering Emotions, Gendering Teams: Construction of Emotions in Self-Managing Teamwork," in Neal M. Ashkanasy, Charmine Hartel, and Wilred Zerbe, eds., *Emotions in the Workplace: Research, Theory and Practice* (Westport, CT: Quorum Books, 2000), 82–96.

80. See Nannerl O. Keohane, "Crossing the Bridge: Reflections on Women and Leadership," in Barbara Kellerman and Deborah L. Rhode, eds., *Women and Leadership* (San Francisco: Jossey-Bass, 2007), 87–88.

81. Todd L. Pittinsky, Laura M. Bacon, and Brian Welle, "The Great Women Theory of Leadership? Perils of Positive Stereotypes and Precarious Pedestals," in Kellerman and Rhode, *Women and Leadership*, 93–125.

Chapter 3

1. Michael Portillo, "Yes, We Will Miss Him; Exit Blair," *International Herald Tribune*, June 23–24, 2007, p. 8.

2. "Follow My Leader: Why Leadership Makes Britons Queasy," *Economist*, October 23, 2004, p. 57.

3. Megan K. Stack, "He Was More Symbol Than Sweeping Leader," *Los Angeles Times*, June 9, 2006, p. 1.

4. Max Weber, "Types of Authority," in Barbara Kellerman, ed., *Political Leadership: A Source Book* (Pittsburgh, PA: University of Pittsburgh Press, 1986), 239. See also Ann Ruth Willner, *The Spellbinders: Charismatic Political Leadership* (New Haven, CT: Yale University Press, 1984).

5. Jay A. Conger and Rabindra N. Kanungo, *Charismatic Leadership in Organizations* (Thousand Oaks, CA: Sage, 1998); see also Gary A. Yukl, "An Evaluation of Conceptual Weaknesses in Transformational and Charismatic Leadership Theories," *Leadership Quarterly* 10, no. 2 (1999): 285–305.

6. Manfred F. R. Kets de Vries, "Origins of Charisma: Ties That Bind the Leaders and the Led," in Jay A. Conger and Rabindra N.

Kanungo, eds., *Charismatic Leadership: The Elusive Factor in Orga-nizational Effectiveness* (San Francisco: Jossey-Bass, 1988), 237–52.

7. Edward Shils, "Charisma, Order, Status," *American Sociological Review* 30 (1965): 199–213.

8. Boas Shamir, "The Charismatic Relationship: Alternative Explanations and Predictions," *Leadership Quarterly* 2, no. 2 (1991): 101.

9. Willner, *The Spellbinders*, 15.

10. See Kets de Vries, "Origins of Charisma"; Jerrold M. Post, *Leaders and Their Followers in a Dangerous World: The Psychology of Political Behavior* (Ithaca, NY: Cornell University Press, 2004), chapter 9.

11. Jennifer O'Connor, Michael D. Mumford, Timothy C. Clifton, Theodore L. Gessner, and Mary Shane Connelly, "Charismatic Leaders and Destructiveness: An Historiometric Study," *Leadership Quarterly* 6, no. 4 (1995): 529–55.

12. Dong I. Jung and John J. Sosik, "Who Are the Spellbinders? Identifying Personal Attributes of Charismatic Leaders," *Journal of Leadership and Organizational Studies* 12, no. 4 (2006): 12–26. See also Jay A. Conger, "Charismatic and Transformational Leadership in Organizations: An Insider's Perspective on These Developing Streams of Research," *Leadership Quarterly* 10, no. 2 (1999): 145–80; Shamir, "The Charismatic Relationship."

13. Dick Morris, quoted in George C. Edwards, *On Deaf Ears: The Limits of the Bully Pulpit* (New Haven, CT: Yale University Press, 2003), 105.

14. Rakesh Khurana, *Searching for a Corporate Savior: The Irrational Quest for Charismatic CEOs* (Princeton, NJ: Princeton University Press, 2002), 75–76.

15. Francis J. Flynn and Barry M. Staw, "Lend Me Your Wallets: The Effect of Charismatic Leadership on External Support for an Organization," *Strategic Management Journal* 25 (2004): 309–30.

16. Rakesh Khurana, "Good Charisma, Bad Business," *New York Times*, September 13, 2002, p. A27.

17. Edwards, *On Deaf Ears*, chapter 4.

18. Alice H. Eagly, Mona G. Makhijani, Richard D. Ashmore, and Laura C. Longo, "What Is Beautiful Is Good, But . . . : A Meta-

Analytic Review of Research on the Physical Attractiveness Stereotype," *Psychological Bulletin* 110, no. 1 (1991): 109–28.

19. "The Politics of Beauty: Fit to Serve," *Economist*, January 20, 2007, p. 71.

20. John D. Mayer, Maria DiPaolo, and Peter Salovey, "Perceiving Affective Content in Ambiguous Visual Stimuli: A Component of Emotional Intelligence," *Journal of Personality Assessment* 54 (1990): 773.

21. Janine Willis and Alexander Todorov, "First Impressions: Making Up Your Mind after a 100-Ms Exposure to a Face," *Psychological Science* 17, no. 7 (2006): 592–98.

22. Daniel J. Benjamin and Jesse M. Shapiro, "Thin Slice Forecasts of Gubernatorial Elections," *Working Paper 12660*, National Bureau of Economic Research, Cambridge, MA, November 2006.

23. Janice M. Beyer, "Taming and Promoting Charisma to Change Organizations," *Leadership Quarterly* 10, no. 2 (1999): 308.

24. Bernard M. Bass, *Transformational Leadership: Industrial, Military, and Educational Impact* (Mahwah, NJ: Lawrence Erlbaum, 1998).

25. Yukl, "An Evaluation of Conceptual Weaknesses," 300.

26. James MacGregor Burns, *Leadership* (New York: Harper & Row, 1978); Bass, *Transformational Leadership*.

27. Bass further divides transactional leaders into active and passive managers by exception in terms of how they monitor compliance with contingent rewards.

28. James Traub, *The Best Intentions: Kofi Annan and the UN in the Era of American World Power* (New York: Farrar, Straus and Giroux, 2006), 15.

29. Daniel Goleman, Richard E. Boyatzis, and Annie McKee, *Primal Leadership: Learning to Lead with Emotional Intelligence* (Boston: Harvard Business School Press, 2002), 44.

30. Timothy A. Judge and Ronald F. Piccolo, "Transformational and Transactional Leadership: A Meta-Analytic Test of Their Relative Validity," *Journal of Applied Psychology* 89, no. 5 (2004): 765.

31. The operational concepts can also be confusing if the dimensions do not co-vary. For a critique, see Yukl, "An Evaluation of Conceptual Weaknesses."

32. Robert A. Caro, *Master of the Senate: The Years of Lyndon Johnson* (New York: Knopf, 2002).

33. James MacGregor Burns, *Transforming Leadership: A New Pursuit of Happiness* (New York: Atlantic Monthly Press, 2003).

34. Richard E. Neustadt, *Presidential Power and the Modern Presidents: The Politics of Leadership from Roosevelt to Reagan* (New York: Free Press, 1990), 10.

35. David G. Winter, "Leader Appeal, Leader Performance, and the Motive Profiles of Leaders and Followers: A Study of American Presidents and Elections," *Journal of Personality and Social Psychology* 52, no. 1 (1989): 196–202; Dean K. Simonton, "Presidential Greatness: The Historical Consensus and Its Psychological Significance," *Political Psychology* 7 (1986): 259–83; and Simonton, "Dispositional Attributions of (Presidential) Leadership: An Experimental Simulation of Historiometric Results," *Journal of Experimental Social Psychology* 22 (1986): 389–418.

36. Qaddafi also said that the need for vision is why he reads books. Personal interview, February 11, 2007.

37. Robert J. Sternberg, "Successful Intelligence: A New Approach to Leadership," in Ronald E. Riggio, Susan E. Murphy, and Francis J. Pirozzolo, eds., *Multiple Intelligences and Leadership* (Mahwah, NJ: Lawrence Erlbaum, 2002), 9–28.

38. Michael D. Mumford and Judy R. Van Doorn, "The Leadership of Pragmatism: Reconsidering Franklin in the Age of Charisma," *Leadership Quarterly* 12, no. 3 (2001): 279–309.

39. Fred I. Greenstein, *The Presidential Difference: Leadership Style from FDR to George W. Bush*, 2nd ed. (Princeton, NJ: Princeton University Press, 2004).

40. Daniel Goleman, "What Makes a Leader?" *Harvard Business Review* 76, no. 6 (1998): 94.

41. John D. Mayer and Peter Salovey, "What Is Emotional Intelligence?" in Peter Salovey and David J. Sluyter, eds., *Emotional Development and Emotional Intelligence: Educational Implications* (New York: Basic Books, 1997), 5.

42. Edward L. Thorndike, "Intelligence and Its Uses," *Harpers Magazine* 140 (1920): 227–35.

43. Greenstein, *The Presidential Difference*, 24.
44. Goleman, "What Makes a Leader?"
45. John D. Mayer, Peter Salovey, and David Caruso, "Models of Emotional Intelligence," in Robert J. Sternberg, ed. *Handbook of Intelligence* (Cambridge, UK: Cambridge University Press, 2000), 412–13.
46. Erving Goffman, *The Presentation of Self in Everyday Life* (Garden City, NY: Doubleday, 1959).
47. "The Man behind the Fist," *Economist*, March 31, 2007, p. 28.
48. Goleman et al., *Primal Leadership*, 28, 33. See also Joyce E. Bono and Remus Ilies, "Charisma, Positive Emotions, and Mood Contagion," *Leadership Quarterly* 17, no. 4 (2006): 330.
49. Michael Ignatieff, "Getting Iraq Wrong: What the War Has Taught Me about Political Judgment," *New York Times Magazine*, August 5, 2007, p. 29.
50. Raymond Hernandez, "On Podium, Some Say, Mrs. Clinton Is No Mr. Clinton," *New York Times*, February 13, 2006, p. B3.
51. I am indebted for this observation to Tom Donilon, personal communication, August 9, 2007.
52. Michelle C. Bligh and Gregory D. Hess, "The Power of Leading Subtly: Alan Greenspan, Rhetorical Leadership, and Monetary Policy," *Leadership Quarterly* 18, no. 2 (2007): 87–104.
53. Dean Williams, *Real Leadership: Helping People and Organizations Face Their Toughest Challenges* (San Francisco: Berrett-Koehler, 2005), chapter 9.
54. Keith Grint, *The Arts of Leadership* (Oxford: Oxford University Press, 2000).
55. Frederick W. Smith, in "All in a Day's Work," *Harvard Business Review*, special issue on *Breakthrough Leadership*, December 2001, p. 57.
56. Paul O'Neill, personal communication, October 2006.
57. Michael Skapinker, "Leadership Shakes Off the Liability of Charisma," *Financial Times*, October 10, 2001, p. 15, reviewing Jim Collins, *Good to Great: Why Some Companies Make the Leap . . . and Others Don't* (New York: Harper Business, 2001).
58. Brent Scowcroft, personal communication, August 3, 2007.

59. Robert Draper, quoted in Michiko Kakutani, "Big Ideas, Tiny Details," *New York Times*, September 5, 2007, p. B10.

60. Annett Conrad, Michael Frohlingsdorf, Konstantin von Hammerstein, Horand Knaup, Felix Kurz, Roland Nelles, Christian Reiermann, Michael Sauga, and Gabor Steingart, "Kanzler im Grauschleier" [Chancellor in Grey Veil], *Der Spiegel*, October 28, 2002, p. 26.

61. Lawrence Bacot, president of Tufts University, personal communication, April 29, 2007.

62. I am indebted to former vice president Al Gore for this formulation. Personal communication, August 3, 2007.

63. When asked, however, whether he could have done more to combat climate change as president than as an outside evangelist, he was clear that the authority of the presidency provided more leverage. Personal communication, August 3, 2007.

64. Andrew Rawnsley, "Tony Blair's Premiership Has Big Lessons for Gordon Brown: Whatever Their Cunning Plans, the Most Tested Times for Leaders Come from the Shock Events They Never Anticipated," *Observer*, June 24, 2007, p. 31.

65. Theodore Roosevelt quoted in James MacGregor Burns and Susan Dunn, *The Three Roosevelts* (New York: Grove Press, 2001), 102.

66. Bob Woodward, *State of Denial* (New York: Simon & Schuster, 2006), 384.

67. Abraham Zaleznik, "Managers and Leaders: Are They Different?" *Harvard Business Review* 55, no. 3 (1977): 67–78.

68. John P. Kotter, *Leading Change* (Boston: Harvard Business School Press, 1996), 58.

69. James G. March, *Primer on Decision Making: How Decisions Happen* (New York: Free Press, 1994), 72.

70. Lawrence B. Wilkerson, "The White House Cabal," *Los Angeles Times*, October 25, 2005, p. B11.

71. Wayne A. Downing, quoted in Thom Shanker, "Study Is Said to Find Overlap in U.S. Counterterror Effort," *New York Times*, March 18, 2006, p. A8.

72. Richard Neustadt, *Presidential Power and the Modern Presidents: The Politics of Leadership from Rosevelt to Reagan* (New York: Free Press, 1990), 221.

73. Fred I. Greenstein, *The Hidden-Hand Presidency: Eisenhower as Leader* (New York: Basic Books, 1982).

74. See David M. Abshire, *Saving the Reagan Presidency: Trust Is the Coin of the Realm* (College Station: Texas A&M University Press, 2005); David R. Gergen, *Eyewitness to Power: The Essence of Leadership: Nixon to Clinton* (New York: Simon & Schuster, 2000).

75. Thomas J. Peters, "Leadership: Sad Facts and Silver," in Daniel Goleman, William Peace, William Pagonis, Tom Peters, Gareth Jones, Harris Collingwood, eds., *Harvard Business Review on Breakthrough Leadership* (Boston: Harvard Business School Press, 2001), 143.

76. Roderick M. Kramer, "The Great Intimidators," *Harvard Business Review* 84, no. 2 (2006): 94.

77. Caro, *Master of the Senate.*

78. "The Man behind the Fist," *Economist*, March 31, 2007, p. 28.

79. David C. McClelland and David H. Burnham, "Power Is the Great Motivator," *Harvard Business Review* 54, no. 2 (2000): 100–110.

80. Michael Harvey, Joyce Heames, and R. Glenn Richey, "Bullying: From the Playground to the Boardroom," *Journal of Leadership and Organizational Studies* 12, no. 4 (2006): 6.

81. Zogby International, "As Labor Day Nears, Workplace Bullying Institute Survey Finds Half of Working Americans Affected by Workplace Bullying," August 39, 2007, http://www.zogby.com/news/ReadNews.dbm?ID=1353.

82. Gerald Feris, Robert Zinko, Robyn Brouer, M. Ronald Buckley, and Michael G. Harvey, "Strategic Bullying as a Supplementary, Balanced Perspective on Destructive Leadership," *Leadership Quarterly* 18, no. 3 (2007): 195–206.

83. Barbara Kellerman, *Bad Leadership: What It Is, How It Happens, Why It Matters* (Boston: Harvard Business School Press, 2004), chapter 7.

84. Katrina Bedell, Samuel Hunter, Amanda Angie, and Andrew Vert, "A Historiometric Examination of Machiavellianism and a New

Taxonomy of Leadership," *Journal of Leadership and Organizational Studies* 12, no. 4 (2006): 50–72; Ronald J. Deluga, "American Presidential Machiavellianism: Implications for Charismatic Leadership and Rated Performance," *Leadership Quarterly* 12 (2001): 339–63.

85. Goleman et al., *Primal Leadership*, 45.

86. Doris Kearns Goodwin, *Team of Rivals: The Political Genius of Abraham Lincoln* (New York: Simon & Schuster, 2005).

87. Kramer, "The Great Intimidators," 91.

88. Jay Lorsch, in "Governing Harvard: A Harvard Magazine Roundtable," *Havard Magazine*, May–June 2006, 31.

89. Here I borrow from categories developed by Fred I. Greenstein, ed., *The George W. Bush Presidency: An Early Assessment* (Baltimore: Johns Hopkins University Press, 2003). He lists cognitive intelligence as the sixth skill, but I have broadened this to a contextual intelligence that is partly analytical and partly intuitive (i.e., based on tacit knowledge).

90. See Marshall Ganz, "Resources and Resourcefulness: Strategic Capacity in the Unionization of California Agriculture, 1959–1966," *American Journal of Sociology* 105, no. 4 (2000): 1010.

Chapter 4

1. Vauhini Vara, "Boss Talks (A Special Report). After GE: Intuit's Steve Bennett on Why Some General Electric Alumni Succeed—and Some Don't," *Wall Street Journal*, April 16, 2007, p. R3.

2. Richard E. Neustadt, *Presidential Power and the Modern Presidents: The Politics of Leadership from Roosevelt to Reagan* (New York: Free Press, 1990), preface; Jameson W. Doig and Erwin C. Hargrove, *Leadership and Innovation: A Biographical Perspective on Entrepreneurs in Government* (Baltimore: Johns Hopkins University Press, 1987), vii.

3. Walesa once commented that he found riot police less terrifying than bureaucrats and budgets. He felt his historical moment as a leader had passed. Personal communication, September 24, 2003.

4. Dean Williams, *Real Leadership: Helping People and Organizations Face Their Toughest Challenges* (San Francisco: Berrett-Koehler, 2005), xiii.

5. Fred E. Fiedler, "The Curious Role of Cognitive Resources in Leadership," in Ronald E. Riggio, Susan E. Murphy, and Francis J. Pirozzolo, eds., *Multiple Intelligences and Leadership* (Mahwah, NJ: Lawrence Erlbaum, 2002), 96, 100.

6. Keith Grint, *The Arts of Leadership* (Oxford: Oxford University Press, 2000), 3.

7. J. Richard Hackman and Ruth Wageman, "When and How Team Leaders Matter," *Research in Organizational Behavior* 26 (2005): 66.

8. Anthony J. Mayo and Nitin Nohria, *In Their Time: The Greatest Business Leaders of the Twentieth Century* (Boston: Harvard Business School Press, 2005).

9. Isaiah Berlin, quoted in Michael Ignatieff, "Getting Iraq Wrong: What the War Has Taught Me about Political Judgment," *New York Times Magazine*, August 5, 2007, p. 28.

10. Alan J. P. Taylor, *Bismarck: The Man and the Statesman* (London: Sutton, 1955), 115.

11. John W. Kingdon, *Agendas, Alternatives, and Public Policies*, 2nd ed. (New York: Longman, 2003), 181.

12. I am indebted to Graham Allison for pointing this out to me.

13. P. Christopher Earley and Soon Ang, *Cultural Intelligence: Individual Interactions across Cultures* (Stanford: Stanford University Press, 2003), 39, 43.

14. Peter Salovey and John D. Mayer, "Emotional Intelligence," *Imagination, Cognition, and Personality* 9 (1990): 185–211; John D. Mayer and Peter Salovey, "The Intelligence of Emotional Intelligence," *Intelligence* 17, no. 4 (1993): 433–42; John D. Mayer and Peter Salovey, "Emotional Intelligence and the Construction and Regulation of Feelings," *Applied and Preventive Psychology* 4 (1995): 197–208; John D. Mayer and Peter Salovey, "What Is Emotional Intelligence?" in Peter Salovey and David Sluyter, eds., *Emotional Development and Emotional Intelligence: Implications for Educators* (New York: Basic Books, 1997), 3–31.

15. Robert J. Sternberg, "Successful Intelligence: A New Approach to Leadership," in Riggio et al., *Multiple Intelligences and Leadership*, 9–28; Fred E. Fiedler, "The Curious Role of Cognitive Resources in Leadership," 96, 101.

16. Nannerl O. Keohane, "On Leadership," *Perspectives on Politics* 3 (2005): 705–22.

17. At some point, for this idea to be a useful scientific concept, social psychologists would have to operationalize it with a reliable, replicable scale that could measure differences in the skill. That is not the task of a primer like this.

18. Michael A. Roberto, *Why Good Leaders Don't Take Yes for an Answer: Managing for Conflict and Consensus* (Upper Saddle River, NJ: Wharton School Publishing, 2005).

19. Michael A. Roberto and Gina M. Carioggia, "Launching the War on Terrorism," *Case No. 9–303–027*, Harvard Business School, Cambridge, MA, 2002, p. 2.

20. Hackman and Wageman, "When and How Team Leaders Matter," 69.

21. Ronald A. Heifetz and Donald L. Laurie, "The Work of Leadership," *Harvard Business Review* 75, no. 1 (1997): 124–34.

22. I am indebted to Dutch Leonard for the bandwidth metaphor.

23. Edgar H. Schein, "Defining Organizational Culture," in J. Thomas Wren, ed., *The Leader's Companion: Insight on Leadership through the Ages* (New York: Free Press, 1995), 281.

24. Earley and Ang, *Cultural Intelligence*, 4–5.

25. Ibid, 11.

26. Sharon Erickson Nepstad and Clifford Bob, "When Do Leaders Matter? Hypotheses on Leadership Dynamics in Social Movements," *Mobilization: An International Journal* 11, no. 1 (2006): 1–22.

27. Kelley Holland, "Life after a Merger: Learning on Both Sides," *New York Times*, June 24, 2007, p. BU21.

28. Daniel Burnham, former CEO of Raytheon, personal interview, December 2006.

29. National Commission on Terrorist Attacks upon the U.S., *9/11 Commission Report: Final Report*, CIS-NO: 2004-J892–23, July 22, 2004, available from http://www.9–11commission.gov/ (retrieved August 31, 2007).

30. Robin J. Ely and Debra E. Meyerson, "Unmasking Manly Men: The Organizational Reconstruction of Men's Identity," *Working Paper No. 07–054*, Harvard Business School, Cambridge, MA, 2007.

31. D. Quinn Mills, "Asian and American Leadership Styles: How Are They Unique?" *Harvard Business School Working Knowledge*, Cambridge, MA, June 27, 2005, p. 6.

32. Geert Hofstede, "Cultural Constraints on Management Theories," in Wren, *The Leader's Companion*, 259, 267.

33. A. Kakabadse, A. Myers, T. McMahon, and G. Spony, "Top Management Styles in Europe: Implications for Business and Cross-National Teams," in Keith Grint, ed., *Leadership: Classical, Contemporary and Critical Approaches* (Oxford: Oxford University Press, 1997), 194.

34. Erna Szabo, Gerhard Reber, Jurgen Weibler, Felix C. Brodbeck, and Rolf Wunderer, "Values and Behavior Orientation in Leadership Studies: Reflections Based on Findings in Three German-Speaking Countries," *Leadership Quarterly* 12 (2001): 219–44.

35. Harry C. Triandis, *Culture and Social Behavior* (New York: McGraw-Hill, 1994); Mansour Javidan and Dale E. Carl, "East Meets West: A Cross Cultural Comparison of Charismatic Leadership among Canadian and Iranian Executives," *Journal of Management Studies* 41, no. 4 (2004): 665–91.

36. Robert J. House, Paul J. Hanges, Mansour Javidan, Peter W. Dorfman, and Vipin Gupta, eds., *Culture, Leadership, and Organizations: The GLOBE Study of 62 Societies* (Thousand Oaks, CA: Sage, 2007).

37. Earley and Ang, *Cultural Intelligence*, 4, 267.

38. Jeswald W. Salacuse, *Leading Leaders: How to Manage Smart, Talented, Rich, and Powerful People* (New York, NY: AMACOM, 2006).

39. Ronald A. Heifetz, "Leadership, Authority, and Women," in Barbara Kellerman and Deborah L. Rhode, eds., *Women and Leadership* (San Francisco: Wiley, 2007), 314–21; and Heifetz, *Leadership without Easy Answers* (Cambridge, MA: Belknap Press of Harvard University Press, 1994).

40. Albert O. Hirschman, *Exit, Voice, and Loyalty: Responses to Decline in Firms, Organizations, and States* (Cambridge, MA: Harvard University Press, 1970).

41. Robert M. Axelrod, *The Evolution of Cooperation* (New York: Basic Books, 1984).

42. Mark H. Moore, *Creating Public Value: Strategic Management in Government* (Cambridge, MA: Harvard University Press, 1995).

43. Heifetz, *Leadership without Easy Answers.*

44. Victor H. Vroom, "Leadership and the Decision Making Process," *Organizational Dynamics* 68 (2000): 82–94.

45. Roberto, *Why Good Leaders Don't Take Yes for an Answer,* chapter 2.

46. He extends the metaphor by asking whether it is an industrial-strength or an ordinary kitchen pressure cooker.

47. David Runciman, "Squalls That Await the New Prime Minister," *Financial Times,* June 28, 2007, p. 13.

48. Jerrold M. Post, *Leaders and Their Followers in a Dangerous World* (Ithaca, NY: Cornell University Press, 2004), 104. See also Gary Klein, *Sources of Power* (Cambridge, MA: MIT Press, 1999); Michael Useem, *The Leadership Moment: Nine True Stories of Triumph and Disaster and Their Lessons for Us All* (New York: Three Rivers Press, 1998).

49. In the terms developed by Graham Allison, relaxing the standard operating procedure constraints described by a Model II analysis may initially help, but if an organization disintegrates to the personal stakes described by his Model III, efficient response may be hindered. See Graham Allison and Philip Zelikow, *Essence of Decision: Explaining the Cuban Missile Crisis,* 2nd ed. (New York: Longman, 1999).

50. Hackman and Wageman, "When and How Team Leaders Matter," 47.

51. Herman B. "Dutch" Leonard and Arnold M. Howitt, "Against Desperate Peril: High Performance in Emergency Preparation and Response," unpublished manuscript.

52. Arnold Howitt and Herman B. Leonard, "Beyond Katrina: Improving Disaster Response Capabilities," part 1, *Crisis Response Journal* 2, no. 3 (2006): 52–53, and part 2, no. 4 (2006): 54–56; Howitt and Leonard, "Katrina and the Core Challenges of Disaster Response," *Fletcher Forum of World Affairs* 30, no. 1 (2006): 215–21.

53. Chester I. Barnard, *The Functions of the Executive* (Cambridge, MA: Harvard University Press, 1979).

54. J. Richard Hackman, *Leading Teams: Setting the Stage for Great Performance* (Boston: Harvard Business School Press, 2002), chapter 4.

55. Mark Landler, "Chairman to Quit Siemens, Casualty in Graft Accusations," *New York Times*, April 20, 2007, p. C3.
56. Col. Edward M. House, quoted in Charles T. Thompson, *The Peace Conference Day by Day: A Presidential Pilgrimage Leading to the Discovery of Europe* (New York: Brentano's, 1920), 190.
57. Lawrence B. Wilkerson, "The White House Cabal," *Los Angeles Times*, October 25, 2005, p. B11.
58. Charles C. Krulak and Joseph P. Hoar, "It's Our Cage, Too," *Washington Post*, May 17, 2007, p. A17.
59. Ben W. Heineman Jr., "Avoiding Integrity Land Mines," *Harvard Business Review* 85, no. 4 (2007): 102.

Chapter 5

1. Dean C. Ludwig and Clinton O. Longenecker, "The Bathsheba Syndrome: The Ethical Failure of Successful Leaders," in Joanne B. Ciulla, ed., *The Ethics of Leadership* (Belmont, CA: Wadsworth, 2003), 70.
2. David C. McClelland and David H. Burnham, "Power Is the Great Motivator," *Harvard Business Review* 54, no. 2 (2000): 100–10. On problems of narcissism, see Seth A. Rosenthal and Todd L. Pittinsky, "Narcissistic Leadership," *Leadership Quarterly* 17, no. 6 (2006): 617–33.
3. Niccolò Machiavelli, *The Prince* (New York: New American Library, 1952).
4. Joseph L. Badaracco Jr., "The Discipline of Building Character," *Harvard Business Review* 76, no. 2 (1998): 114–24.
5. James MacGregor Burns, *Leadership* (New York: Harper & Row, 1978).
6. "Saddam Hussein: The Blundering Dictator," *Economist*, January 6, 2007, pp. 39–40; "Slobodan Milosevic," *Economist*, March 18, 2006, p. 83.
7. C. J. Chivers, "Behold Turkmenistan's Marvels! (Authorized Version)," *New York Times*, July 19, 2007, p. A4.
8. See, for example, the special issue devoted to "destructive leadership" of *Leadership Quarterly* 18, no. 3 (2007).

9. Barbara Kellerman, *Bad Leadership: What It Is, How It Happens, Why It Matters* (Boston: Harvard Business School Press, 2004). Kellerman may be too harsh on Meeker, who persisted despite initial failure and went on to redemption in a continuing career as an analyst.

10. Ibid.

11. Terry L. Price, "Explaining Ethical Failures of Leadership," in Joanne B. Ciulla, ed., *Ethics, the Heart of Leadership*, 2nd ed. (Westport, CT: Praeger, 2004), 144.

12. Kellerman criticizes Clinton as intemperate, but some critics were more disturbed by his cover-up and lies under oath in court than by his intemperate actions themselves. Others excused the public lies because they were about private sexual behavior and designed to protect his family.

13. S. Alexander Haslam and Michael J. Platow, "The Link between Leadership and Followership: How Affirming Social Identity Translates Vision into Action," *Personality and Social Psychology Bulletin* 27, no. 11 (2001): 1471.

14. The term comes from the title of a play *Dirty Hands* by Jean Paul Sartre in which a seasoned revolutionary tells a young political activist who insists on maintaining his purity that purity is "a pretext for doing nothing. . . . I have dirty hands. Right up to the elbows. I've plunged them in filth and blood. . . . Do you think you can govern innocently?"

15. The problem of dirty hands has had various formulations. Joseph Badaracco describes it in terms of conflicting moral principles, or "right vs. right." See his *Defining Moments: When Managers Must Choose between Right and Right* (Boston: Harvard Business School Press, 1997). I focus more on the trade-off between principles and consequences and the tragic choices that arise because there is "no single standard that renders all moral values commensurable." See Kenneth Winston, "Necessity and Choice in Political Ethics: Varieties of Dirty Hands," in Daniel E. Wueste, ed., *Professional Ethics and Social Responsibility* (Lanham, MD: Rowman and Littlefield, 1994), 37–66. Gerald F. Gaus tries to dissolve this problem, but I do not regard his as a satisfactory solution. See "Dirty Hands," in R. G. Frey and Christopher Heath Wellman,

eds., *A Companion to Applied Ethics* (Malden, MA: Blackwell, 2003), 167–79.

16. Michael Walzer, "Political Action: The Problem of Dirty Hands," *Philosophy and Public Affairs* 2, no. 2 (1973): 164.

17. One problem with this familiar example is that it assumes the efficacy of torture in producing reliable intelligence.

18. Kenneth Winston disagrees with Walzer's formulation and sees dirty hands as a conflict of moral standards in the public sphere. See Winston, "Necessity and Choice." I am grateful for his personal communication of this issue with me.

19. Max Weber, "Politics as a Vocation," in H. H. Gerth and C. Wright Mills, eds., *From Max Weber: Essays in Sociology* (New York: Oxford University Press, 1958), 126.

20. This is an adaptation of "Jim in the Jungle," an example constructed by Bernard Williams, *Moral Luck* (Cambridge, UK: Cambridge University Press, 1981), 43.

21. As it happens, I would drop the gun because I would not trust the commander to keep his word, but that does escape the basic dilemma of the example.

22. Benedict Carey, "Brain Injury Said to Affect Moral Choices," *New York Times*, March 22, 2007, p. A19.

23. "Philosophy and Neuroscience: Posing the Right Question," *Economist*, March 24, 2007, p. 92.

24. I am obliged to Kenneth Winston for these distinctions in a personal correspondence, October 2006.

25. Isaiah Berlin, "Two Concepts of Liberty," in *Liberty: Incorporating Four Essays on Liberty*, edited by Henry Hardy (New York: Oxford University Press, 1969), 168.

26. Egil Krogh, "The Break-in That History Forgot," *New York Times*, June 30, 2007, p. A17.

27. See Jonathan Bennett, "The Conscience of Huckleberry Finn," 81–91, and Hannah Arendt, "The Accused and Duties of a Law-Abiding Citizen," 122, in Ciulla, *The Ethics of Leadership*.

28. Joseph Badaracco, *Defining Moments*, 51.

29. This example is borrowed from a lecture by Amartya Sen, Harvard University, May 2007.

30. Graham T. Allison and Lance M. Liebman, "Lying in Office," in Amy Gutmann and Dennis Thompson, eds., *Ethics and Politics: Cases and Comments*, 2nd ed. (Chicago: Nelson-Hall, 1990), 41.

31. Cathal J. Nolan, "'Bodyguard of Lies': Franklin D. Roosevelt and Defensible Deceit in World War II," in Cathal J. Nolan, ed., *Ethics and Statecraft: The Moral Dimensions of International Affairs*, 2nd ed. (Westport, CT: Praeger, 2004), 35.

32. Allison and Liebman, "Lying in Office," 40.

33. Eric Alterman, *When Presidents Lie: A History of Official Deception and Its Consequences* (New York: Viking, 2004), 314. See also Carl Cannon, "Untruth and Consequences," *The Atlantic*, January–February 2007, 56–67.

34. Geoff Mulgan, "We Need Government—and We Need It to Be Boring," *Spectator*, May 13, 2006, p. 17.

35. Of course, there are many forms of participation. See, for example, Archon Fung and Erik Olin Wright, eds., *Deepening Democracy: Institutional Innovations in Empowered Participatory Governance* (London: Verso, 2003).

36. For a gripping example, see the account in Jon Krakauer, *Into Thin Air: A Personal Account of the Mt. Everest Disaster* (New York: Villard, 1998).

37. Williams, *Moral Luck*, 26.

38. Enoch Powell, quoted in Jairam Ramesh, "Political Legacies," *Economist*, June 23, 2007, p. 21.

39. Philip Stephens, "Hubris Is the Thread Running through Blair's Many Travails," *Financial Times*, July 14, 2006, p. 15.

40. James Hershberg, quoted in Michael Abramowitz, "Truman's Trials Resonate for Bush," *Washington Post*, December 15, 2006, p. A3.

41. David Brooks, "Heroes and History," *New York Times*, July 17, 2007, p. A21.

42. Abramowitz, "Truman's Trials Resonate."

43. For an alternative view that likes the odds, see William Kristol, "Why Bush Will Be a Winner," *Washington Post*, July 15, 2007, p. B1.

44. The same poll showed that Bush trailed Nixon as the modern president with the highest negative ratings.

45. Zogby International, "Roosevelt Continues to Dominate Presidential Greatness Scale," http://www.zogby.com/news/Read News.dbm?ID=1234 (retrieved August 31, 2007).

46. Burns, *Leadership*, 20.

47. Michael Keeley, "The Trouble with Transformational Leadership: Toward a Federalist Ethic for Organizations," in Ciulla, *Ethics: The Heart of Leadership*, 159.

48. Ibid, 166–67.

49. Louise Tourigny, William L. Dougan, John Washbush, and Christine Clements, "Explaining Executive Integrity: Governance, Charisma, Personality and Agency," *Management Decisions* 41, no. 10 (2003): 1043.

50. Ibid, 1041.

51. Russell Hardin, "Morals for Public Officials," in Deborah L. Rhode, ed., *Moral Leadership: The Theory and Practice of Power, Judgment, and Policy* (San Francisco: Jossey-Bass, 2006), 116–17.

52. Ben W. Heineman Jr., "Avoiding Integrity Land Mines," *Harvard Business Review* 85, no. 4 (2007): 102.

53. Philip G. Zimbardo, "The Psychology of Power: To the Person? To the Situation? To the System?" in Rhode, *Moral Leadership*, 153.

54. Joel Podolny, Rakesh Khurana, and Marya Hill-Popper, "Revisiting the Meaning of Leadership," unpublished paper, 2004.

55. Deborah Ancona, Thomas W. Malone, Wanda J. Orlikowski, and Peter M. Senge, "In Praise of the Incomplete Leader," *Harvard Business Review* 85, no. 2 (2007): 95.

56. Craig Lambert, "Le Professeur," *Harvard Magazine*, July–August 2007, p. 37.

57. Keith Grint, *The Arts of Leadership* (Oxford: Oxford University Press, 2000), 406. See also Stephen L. Lilley and Gerald M. Platt, "Correspondents' Images of Martin Luther King, Jr: An Interpretive Theory of Movement Leadership," reprinted in Keith Grint, ed. *Leadership: Classical, Contemporary, and Critical Approaches* (Oxford: Oxford University Press, 1997), 319–37.

58. Haslam and Platow, "The Link between Leadership and Followership," 1471.

59. Todd L Pittinsky, "Allophilia and Intergroup Leadership," in Nancy S. Huber and Mark C. Walker, eds., *Building Leadership Bridges 2005: Emergent Models of Global Leadership* (Collge Park, MD: International Leadership Association, 2005), 34–49.

60. Howard Gardner, "Leadership: A Cognitive Perspective," *SAIS Review* 16, no. 2 (1996): 121.

61. Judith M. Brown, *Nehru: A Political Life* (New Haven, CT: Yale University Press, 2003), 203.

62. Peggy Noonan, "What Nobodies Know," *Wall Street Journal*, March 23, 2006, http://www.opinionjournal.com/columnists/pnoonan/?id=110008126 (retrieved August 31, 2007).

63. Benedict Anderson, *Imagined Communities: Reflections on the Origin and Spread of Nationalism*, rev. ed. (New York: Verso, 1991).

64. See Samantha Power, *"A Problem from Hell": America and the Age of Genocide* (New York: Basic Books, 2002).

65. There is a large literature on the subject, but it is interesting to note that the leading liberal philosopher, John Rawls, chose not to apply his theory of justice in a cosmopolitan manner. See his *Law of Peoples* (Cambridge, MA: Harvard University Press, 1999).

66. Kwame Anthony Appiah, *The Ethics of Identity* (Princeton, NJ: Princeton University Press, 2005), 235.

67. See Barbara Kellerman, *Followership: How Followers Are Creating Change and Changing Leaders* (Boston: Harvard Business School Press, forthcoming).

68. This is an adaptation of Robert E. Kelley, "In Praise of Followers," *Harvard Business Review* 66 (1988): 142–48; and Kelley, *The Power of Followership: How to Create Leaders People Want to Follow, and Followers Who Lead Themselves* (New York: Doubleday/Currency, 1992), 97.

69. For example, Amy C. Edmondson found that implementation of new technology in operating rooms succeeded better when power and status were minimized and team members spoke up. "Speaking Up in the Operating Room: How Team Leaders Promote Learning in Interdisciplinary Action Teams," *Journal of Management Studies* 40, no. 6 (2003): 1419.

70. See Yael Lapidot, Ronit Kark, and Boas Shamir, "The Impact of Situational Vulnerability on the Development and Erosion of

Followers' Trust in Their Leader," *Leadership Quarterly* 18, no. 1 (2007): 16–34.

71. The anecdote is in Kelley, *The Power of Followership*, 230.

72. Brown, *Nehru*, 343.

73. Albert O. Hirschman, *Exit, Voice, and Loyalty: Responses to Decline in Firms, Organizations, and States* (Cambridge, MA: Harvard University Press, 1970).

74. I am indebted to Mark Fliegauf for this insight.

75. James G. Blight and Janet M. Lang, *The Fog of War: Lessons from the Life of Robert S. McNamara* (Lanham, MD: Rowman & Littlefield, 2005).

76. See Edward Weisband and Thomas M. Franck, *Resignation in Protest: Political and Ethical Choices between Loyalty to Team and Loyalty to Conscience in American Public Life* (New York: Penguin Books, 1975).

77. I explore the moral issues of leaking in a life-and-death case in *The Power Game: A Washington Novel* (New York: Public Affairs, 2004).

78. Frances J. Milliken, Elizabeth W. Morrison, and Patricia F. Hewlin, "An Exploratory Study of Employee Silence: Issues That Employees Don't Communicate Upward and Why," *Journal of Management Studies* 40 (2003): 1453–76. See also Chris Argyris, "Double Loop Learning in Organizations," *Harvard Business Review* 55, no. 5 (1977): 115–29.

79. Richard Armitage, quoted in Richard N. Haass, *The Bureaucratic Entrepreneur: How to Be Effective in Any Unruly Organization* (Washington, DC: Brookings Institution Press, 1999), 40.

80. See Mark H. Moore, *Creating Public Value: Strategic Management in Government* (Cambridge, MA: Harvard University Press, 1995).

81. Karl W. Deutsch observed that possessing power was an opportunity not to learn. See *The Nerves of Government: Models of Political Communication and Control* (New York: Free Press, 1966), 111. I am indebted to Mark Moore for pointing this out. (The exact quote: "Power in this narrow sense is the priority of output over intake, the ability to talk instead of listen. In a sense, it is the ability to afford not to learn.")

82. Determining such degrees of choice can become a legal issue. When a young woman accused the Mormon polygymist leader

Warren Jeffs of forcing her into a marriage because she had been taught to obey her religious leaders or "forfeit our chance at the afterlife," determining how much control that gave Jeffs became a crucial legal question. John Dougherty, "'Jane Doe' Testifies as Trial of Polygymist Leader Begins," *New York Times*, September 14, 2007.

83. Lao Tzu, *Tao Te Ching: A New English Version*, with foreword and notes by Stephen Mitchell (London: Macmillan, 1988), 19.

84. McClelland and Burnham, "Power Is the Great Motivator," 11.

85. David Stauffer, "Boosting Your Emotional Intelligence," *Harvard Management Update* 2, no. 10 (1997): 3–4.

86. Chris Argyris, "Teaching Smart People How to Learn," *Harvard Business Review* 69, no. 3 (1991): 99–109.

Bibliography

Articles and Chapters

Allison, Graham T., and Lance M. Liebman. "Lying in Office." In *Ethics and Politics: Cases and Comments*, edited by Amy Gutmann and Dennis Thompson, 40–45. 2nd ed. Chicago: Nelson-Hall, 1990.

Allison, Scott T., and Dafna Eylon. "The Demise of Leadership: Death Positivity Biases in Posthumous Impressions of Leaders." In *The Psychology of Leadership: New Perspectives and Research*, edited by David M. Messick and Roderick M. Kramer, 295–317. Mahwah, NJ: Lawrence Erlbaum, 2005.

Ames, Daniel R., and Francis J. Flynn. "What Breaks a Leader: The Curvilinear Relation between Assertiveness and Leadership." *Journal of Personality and Social Psychology* 92, no. 2 (2007): 307–24.

Ancona, Deborah, Thomas W. Malone, Wanda J. Orlikowski, and Peter M. Senge. "In Praise of the Incomplete Leader." *Harvard Business Review* 85, no. 2 (2007): 92–100.

Arendt, Hannah. "The Accused and Duties of a Law-Abiding Citizen." In *The Ethics of Leadership*, edited by Joanne B. Ciulla, 119–23. Belmont, CA: Wadsworth, 2003.

Argyris, Chris. "Double Loop Learning in Organizations." *Harvard Business Review* 55, no. 5 (1977): 115–29.

———. "Teaching Smart People How to Learn." *Harvard Business Review* 69, no. 3 (1991): 99–109.

Arvey, Richard D., Maria Rotundo, Wendy Johnson, Zhen Zhang, and Matt McGue. "The Determinants of Leadership Role Occupancy: Genetic and Personality Factors." *Leadership Quarterly* 17, no. 1 (2006): 1–20.

Bachrach, Peter, and Morton S. Baratz. "Decisions and Nondecisions: An Analytical Framework." *American Political Science Review* 57, no. 3 (1963): 632–42.

Badaracco, Jr., Joseph L. "The Discipline of Building Character." *Harvard Business Review* 76, no. 2 (1998): 114–24.

Baldwin, David. "The Costs of Power." *Journal of Conflict Resolution* 15, no. 2 (1971): 145–55.

———. "Power Analysis and World Politics: New Trends versus Old Tendencies." *World Politics* 31, no. 2 (1979): 161–94.

Bedell, Katrina, Samuel Hunter, Amanda Angie, and Andrew Vert. "A Historiometric Examination of Machiavellianism and a New Taxonomy of Leadership." *Journal of Leadership and Organizational Studies* 12, no. 4 (2006): 50–72.

Benjamin, Daniel J., and Jesse M. Shapiro. "Thin Slice Forecasts of Gubernatorial Elections." *Working Paper 12660* (November 2006). Cambridge, MA: National Bureau of Economic Research.

Bennett, Jonathan. "The Conscience of Huckleberry Finn." In *The Ethics of Leadership*, edited by Joanne B. Ciulla, 81–91. Belmont, CA: Wadsworth, 2003.

Bennis, Warren G. "Where Have All the Leaders Gone?" *Technology Review* 79 (1977): 3–12.

Berlin, Isaiah. "Two Concepts of Liberty." In Isaiah Berlin, *Liberty: Incorporating Four Essays on Liberty*, edited by Henry Hardy, 166–217. New York: Oxford University Press, 1969.

Beyer, Janice M. "Taming and Promoting Charisma to Change Organizations." *Leadership Quarterly* 10, no. 2 (1999): 307–30.

Bligh, Michelle C., and Gregory D. Hess. "The Power of Leading Subtly: Alan Greenspan, Rhetorical Leadership, and Monetary Policy." *Leadership Quarterly* 18, no. 2 (2007): 87–104.

Bligh, Michelle C., and James R. Meindl. "The Cultural Ecology of Leadership: An Analysis of Popular Leadership Books." In *The Psychology of Leadership: New Perspectives and Research*, edited by David

M. Messick and Roderick M. Kramer, 11–52. Mahwah, NJ: Lawrence Erlbaum, 2005.

Bob, Clifford, and Sharon Erickson Nepstad. "Kill a Leader, Murder a Movement? Leadership and Assassination in Social Movements." *American Behavioral Scientist* 50, no. 10 (2007): 1370–94.

Bono, Joyce E., and Remus Ilies. "Charisma, Positive Emotions, and Mood Contagion." *Leadership Quarterly* 17, no. 4 (2006): 317–34.

Bowles, Hannah Riley, and Kathleen L. McGinn. "Claiming Authority: Negotiating Challenges for Women Leaders." In *The Psychology of Leadership: New Perspectives and Research*, edited by David M. Messick and Roderick M. Kramer, 191–208. Mahwah, NJ: Lawrence Erlbaum, 2005.

Brass, Daniel J. "Men's and Women's Networks: A Study of Interaction Patterns and Influence in an Organization." *Academy of Management Journal* 28, no. 2 (1985): 327–43.

Brass, Daniel J., and David Krackhardt. "The Social Capital of Twenty-First Century Leaders." In *Out-of-the-Box Leadership Challenges for the 21st Century Army and Other Top-Performing Organizations*, edited by James G. Hunt, George E. Dodge, and Leonard Wong, 179–94. Stamford, CT: Jai Press, 1999.

Brown, Michael E., and Dennis A. Gioia. "Making Things Click: Distributive Leadership in an Online Division of an Offline Organization." *Leadership Quarterly* 13, no. 4 (2002): 397–419.

Bryman, Alan. "Leadership in Organizations." In *Handbook of Organization Studies*, edited by Stewart Clegg, Cynthia Hardy, and Walter Nord, 276–92. London: Sage, 1996.

Carlyle, Thomas. "The Leader as Hero." In *Political Leadership: A Source Book*, edited by Barbara Kellerman, 5–9. Pittsburgh, PA: University of Pittsburgh Press, 1986.

Cassell, Justine, David Huffaker, Dona Tversky, and Kim Ferriman. "The Language of Online Leadership: Gender and Youth Engagement on the Internet." *Developmental Psychology* 42, no. 3 (2006): 436–49.

Ciulla, Joanne B. "Leadership Ethics: Mapping the Territory." In *Ethics: The Heart of Leadership*, edited by Joanne B. Ciulla, 3–24. 2nd ed. Westport, CT: Praeger, 2004.

Conger, Jay A. "Charismatic and Transformational Leadership in Organizations: An Insider's Perspective on These Developing Streams of Research." *Leadership Quarterly* 10, no. 2 (1999): 145–80.

Conger, Jay A., and Craig L. Pearce. "A Landscape of Opportunities: Future Research on Shared Leadership." In *Shared Leadership: Reframing the Hows and Whys of Leadership*, edited by Craig L. Pearce and Jay A. Conger, 285–304. Thousand Oaks, CA: Sage, 2003.

Deluga, Ronald J. "American Presidential Machiavellianism: Implications for Charismatic Leadership and Rated Performance." *Leadership Quarterly* 12, no. 3 (2001): 339–63.

Eagly, Alice H., and Blair T. Johnson. "Gender and Leadership Style: A Meta-Analysis." *Psychological Bulletin* 108 (1990): 233–56.

Eagly, Alice H., Mona G. Makhijani, Richard D. Ashmore, and Laura C. Longo. "What Is Beautiful Is Good, but . . . : A Meta-Analytic Review of Research on the Physical Attractiveness Stereotype." *Psychological Bulletin* 110, no. 1 (1991): 109–28.

Edmondson, Amy C. "Speaking Up in the Operating Room: How Team Leaders Promote Learning in Interdisciplinary Action Teams." *Journal of Management Studies* 40, no. 6 (2003): 1419–52.

Ely, Robin J., and Debra E. Meyerson. "Unmasking Manly Men: The Organizational Reconstruction of Men's Identity." *Working Paper No. 07–054.* Cambridge, MA: Harvard Business School, 2007.

Evans, Philip, and Bob Wolf. "Collaboration Rules." *Harvard Business Review* 83, no. 7 (2005): 96–104.

Ferris, Gerald R., Robert Zinko, Robin L. Brouer, M. Ronald Buckley, and Michael G. Harvey. "Strategic Bullying as a Supplementary, Balanced Perspective on Destructive Leadership." *Leadership Quarterly* 18, no. 3 (2007): 195–206.

Fiedler, Fred E. "The Curious Role of Cognitive Resources in Leadership." In *Multiple Intelligences and Leadership*, edited by Ronald E. Riggio, Susan E. Murphy, and Francis J. Pirozzolo, 91–104. Mahwah, NJ: Lawrence Erlbaum, 2002.

Fletcher, Joyce K. "The Paradox of Postheroic Leadership: An Essay on Gender, Power, and Transformational Change." *Leadership Quarterly* 15, no. 5 (2004): 647–61.

Flynn, Francis J., and Barry M. Staw. "Lend Me Your Wallets: The Effect of Charismatic Leadership on External Support for an Organization." *Strategic Management Journal* 25 (2004): 309–30.

French, John R. P., and Bertram H. Raven. "The Bases of Social Power." In *Studies in Social Power*, edited by Dorwin Cartwright, 150–67. Ann Arbor, MI: Institute of Social Research, 1959.

Galinsky, Adam, Joe C. Magee, M. Ena Inesi, and Deborah Gruenfeld. "Power and Perspectives Not Taken." *Psychological Science* 17, no. 12 (2006): 1068–74.

Ganz, Marshall. "Resources and Resourcefulness: Strategic Capacity in the Unionization of California Agriculture, 1959–1966." *The American Journal of Sociology* 105, no. 4 (2000): 1003–62.

Gardner, Howard. "Leadership: A Cognitive Perspective." *SAIS Review* 16, no. 2 (1996): 109–22.

Gaus, Gerald F. "Dirty Hands." In *A Companion to Applied Ethics*, edited by R.G. Frey and Christopher Heath Wellman, 167–79. Malden, MA: Blackwell, 2003.

George, Bill, Peter Sims, Andrew N. McLean, and Diana Mayer. "Discovering Your Authentic Leadership." *Harvard Business Review* 85, no. 2 (2007): 129–38.

Goleman, Daniel. "What Makes a Leader?" *Harvard Business Review* 76, no. 6 (1998): 93–102.

Granovetter, Mark. "The Myth of Social Network Analysis as a Special Method in the Social Sciences." *Connections* 13, no. 2 (1990): 13–16.

Grant, Ruth W. "Ethics and Incentives: A Political Approach." *American Political Science Review* 100, no. 1 (2006): 29–39.

Groysberg, Boris, Andrew N. McLean, and Nitin Nohria. "Are Leaders Portable?" *Harvard Business Review* 84, no. 5 (2006): 92–100.

Hackman, J. Richard. "Rethinking Team Leadership or Team Leaders Are Not Music Directors." In *The Psychology of Leadership: New Persepctives and Research*, edited by David M. Messick and Roderick M. Kramer, 115–42. Mahwah, NJ: Lawrence Erlbaum, 2005.

Hackman, J. Richard, and Ruth Wageman. "When and How Team Leaders Matter." *Research in Organizational Behavior* 26 (2005): 37–74.

Hardin, Russell. "Morals for Public Officials." In *Moral Leadership: The Theory and Practice of Power, Judgment, and Policy,* edited by Deborah L. Rhode, 111–25. San Francisco: Jossey-Bass, 2006.

Harvey, Michael G., Joyce T. Heames, R. Glenn Richey, and Nancy Leonard. "Bullying: From the Playground to the Boardroom." *Journal of Leadership and Organizational Studies* 12, no. 4 (2006): 1–11.

Haslam, S. Alexander, and Michael J. Platow. "The Link between Leadership and Followership: How Affirming Social Identity Translates Vision Into Action." *Personality and Social Psychology Bulletin* 27, no. 11 (2001): 1469–79.

Heifetz, Ronald A. "Leadership, Authority, and Women." In *Women and Leadership,* edited by Barbara Kellerman and Deborah L. Rhode, 311–27. San Francisco: John Wiley & Sons, 2007.

———. "The Scholarly/Practical Challenge of Leadership." In *Reflections on Leadership,* edited by Richard A. Couto, 31–44. Lanham, MD: University Press of America, 2007.

Heifetz, Ronald A., and Donald L. Laurie. "The Work of Leadership." *Harvard Business Review* 75, no. 1 (1997): 124–34.

Heineman, Jr., Ben W. "Avoiding Integrity Land Mines." *Harvard Business Review* 85, no. 4 (2007): 100–108.

Hofstede, Geert. "Cultural Constraints on Management Theories." In *The Leader's Companion: Insight on Leadership through the Ages,* edited by J. Thomas Wren, 253–70. New York: Free Press, 1995.

Hook, Sidney. "The Eventful Man and the Event-Making Man." In *Political Leadership: A Source Book,* edited by Barbara Kellerman, 24–35. Pittsburgh, PA: University of Pittsburgh Press, 1986.

Howitt, Arnold, and Herman B. Leonard. "Beyond Katrina: Improving Disaster Response Capabilities." *Crisis Response Journal* 2, no. 3, and 2, no. 4 (2006): 52–53, and 54–56.

———. "Katrina and the Core Challenges of Disaster Response." *The Fletcher Forum of World Affairs* 30, no. 1 (2006): 215–21.

Hume, David. "Of the First Principles of Government." In *Essays Moral, Political and Literary,* edited by Eugene F. Miller, 32–36. Indianapolis, IN: Liberty Classics, 1985.

Ibarra, Herminia. "Personal Networks of Women and Minorities in Management: A Conceptual Framework." *The Academy of Management Review* 18, no. 1 (1993): 56–87.

Javidan, Mansour, and Dale E. Carl. "East Meets West: A Cross Cultural Comparison of Charismatic Leadership among Canadian and Iranian Executives." *Journal of Management Studies* 41, no. 4 (2004): 665–91.

Judge, Timothy A., and Ronald F. Piccolo. "Transformational and Transactional Leadership; A Meta-Analytic Test of Their Relative Validity." *Journal of Applied Psychology* 89, no. 5 (2004): 755–68.

Jung, Dong I., and John J. Sosik. "Who Are the Spellbinders? Identifying Personal Attributes of Charismatic Leaders." *Journal of Leadership and Organizational Studies* 12, no. 4 (2006): 12–26.

Kakabadse, Andrew, A. Myers, T. McMahon, and G. Spony. "Top Management Styles in Europe: Implications for Business and Cross-National Teams." In *Leadership: Classical, Contemporary and Critical Approaches*, edited by Keith Grint, 179–98. Oxford: Oxford University Press, 1997.

Keeley, Michael. "The Trouble with Transformational Leadership: Toward a Federalist Ethic for Organizations." In *Ethics: The Heart of Leadership*, edited by Joanne B. Ciulla, 149–74. 2nd ed. Westport, CT: Praeger, 2004.

Kelley, Robert E. "In Praise of Followers." *Harvard Business Review* 66 (1988): 142–48.

Keohane, Nannerl O. "On Leadership." *Perspectives on Politics* 3 (2005): 705–22.

———. "Crossing the Bridge: Reflections on Women and Leadership." In *Women and Leadership*, edited by Barbara Kellerman and Deborah L. Rhode, 65–91. San Francisco: Jossey-Bass, 2007.

Kets de Vries, Manfred F. R. "Origins of Charisma: Ties That Bind the Leaders and the Led." In *Charismatic Leadership: The Elusive Factor in Organizational Effectiveness*, edited by Jay A. Conger and Rabindra N. Kanungo, 237–52. San Francisco: Jossey-Bass, 1988.

Knauft, Bruce M. "Violence and Sociality in Human Evolution." *Current Anthropology* 32, no. 4 (1991): 391–428.

Kramer, Roderick M. "The Great Intimidators." *Harvard Business Review* 84, no. 2 (2006): 88–96.

Lapidot, Yael, Ronit Kark, and Boas Shamir. "The Impact of Situational Vulnerability on the Development and Erosion of Followers' Trust in their Leader." *Leadership Quarterly* 18, no. 1 (2007): 16–34.

Lehmann, E. V., and J. Richard Hackman. "Nobody on the Podium: Lessons for Leaders from the Orpheus Chamber Orchestra." Case No. 1644.9. Cambridge, MA: John F. Kennedy School of Government, Harvard University, 2002.

Leonard, Herman B. "Dutch," and Arnold M. Howitt. "Against Desperate Peril: High Performance in Emergency Preparation and Response." Forthcoming.

Lieberson, Stanley, and James F. O'Connor. "Leadership and Organizational Performance: A Study of Large Corporations." *American Sociological Review* 37, no. 2 (1972): 117–30.

Lilley, Stephen L., and Gerald M. Platt. "Correspondents' Images of Martin Luther King, Jr: An Interpretive Theory of Movement Leadership." In *Leadership: Classical, Contemporary, and Critical Approaches*, edited by Keith Grint, 319–37. Oxford: Oxford University Press, 1997.

Locke, Edwin. "Leadership Starting at the Top." In *Shared Leadership: Reframing the Hows and Whys of Leadership*, edited by Craig L. Pearce and Jay A. Conger, 269–84. Thousand Oaks, CA: Sage, 2003.

Ludwig, Dean C., and Clinton O. Longenecker. "The Bathsheba Syndrome: The Ethical Failure of Successful Leaders." In *The Ethics of Leadership,* edited by Joanne B. Ciulla, 70–81. Belmont, CA: Wadsworth, 2003.

March, James G. "The Power of Power." In *Varieties of Political Theory*, edited by David Easton, 39–70. Englewood Cliffs, NJ: Prentice-Hall, 1966.

Mattern, Janice Bially. "Why Soft Power Isn't So Soft: Representational Force and the Sociolinguistic Construction of Attraction in World Politics." *Millennium* 33, no. 3 (2005): 583–612.

Mayer, John D., Maria DiPaolo, and Peter Salovey. "Perceiving Affective Content in Ambiguous Visual Stimuli: A Component of Emotional Intelligence." *Journal of Personality Assessment* 54 (1990): 772–81.

Mayer, John D., and Peter Salovey. "The Intelligence of Emotional Intelligence." *Intelligence* 17, no. 4 (1993): 433–42.

———. "Emotional Intelligence and the Construction and Regulation of Feelings." *Applied and Preventive Psychology* 4 (1995): 197–208.

———. "What is Emotional Intelligence?" In *Emotional Development and Emotional Intelligence: Educational Implications*, edited by Peter Salovey and David J. Sluyter, 3–31. New York: Basic Books, 1997.

Mayer, John D., Peter Salovey, and David Caruso. "Models of Emotional Intelligence." In *Handbook of Intelligence*, edited by Robert J. Sternberg, 386–420. Cambridge: Cambridge University Press, 2000.

McClelland, David C., and David H. Burnham. "Power Is the Great Motivator." *Harvard Business Review* 54, no. 2 (2000): 100–110.

Meindl, James R., Sanford B. Erhlich, and Janet M. Dukeich. "The Romance of Leadership." *Administrative Science Quarterly* 30 (1985): 78–102.

Milliken, Frances J., Elizabeth W. Morrison, and Patricia F. Hewlin. "An Exploratory Study of Employee Silence: Issues That Employees Don't Communicate Upward and Why." *Journal of Management Studies* 40 (2003): 1453–76.

Mills, D. Quinn. "Asian and American Leadership Styles: How Are They Unique?" *Harvard Business School Working Knowledge*, June 27, 2005.

Mobius, Markus M., and Tanja S. Rosenblat. "Why Beauty Matters." *American Economic Review* 96, no. 1 (2006): 222–35.

Mumford, Michael D., and Judy R. Van Doorn. "The Leadership of Pragmatism. Reconsidering Franklin in the Age of Charisma." *Leadership Quarterly* 12, no. 3 (2001): 279–309.

Nepstad, Sharon Erickson, and Clifford Bob. "When Do Leaders Matter? Hypotheses on Leadership Dynamics in Social Movements." *Mobilization: An International Journal* 11, no. 1 (2006): 1–22.

Nolan, Cathal J. "'Bodyguard of Lies': Franklin D. Roosevelt and Defensible Deceit in World War II." In *Ethics and Statecraft: The Moral Dimensions of International Affairs*, edited by Cathal J. Nolan, 35–58. 2nd ed. Westport, CT: Praeger, 2004.

O'Connor, Jennifer, Michael D. Mumford, Timothy C. Clifton, Theodore L. Gessner, and Mary Shane Connelly. "Charismatic

Leaders and Destructiveness: An Historiometric Study." *Leadership Quarterly* 6, no. 4 (1995): 529–55.

Oh, Paul S., and David E. Lewis. "Management and Leadership Performance in the Defense Department: Evidence from Surveys of Federal Employees." *Armed Forces and Society*, forthcoming.

Ollilainen, Marjukka. "Gendering Emotions, Gendering Teams: Construction of Emotions in Self-Managing Teamwork." In *Emotions in the Workplace: Research, Theory and Practice*, edited by Neal M. Ashkanasy, Charmine Hartel, and Wilred Zerbe, 82–96. Westport, CT: Quorum Books, 2000.

O'Mahony, Siobhan. "Governance in Production Communities." Unpublished manuscript, 2007.

O'Toole, James, Jay Galbraith, and Edward E. Lawler III. "The Promise and Pitfalls of Shared Leadership: When Two (or More) Heads Are Better Than One." In *Shared Leadership: Reframing the Hows and Whys of Leadership*, edited by Craig L. Pearce and Jay A. Conger, 250–68. Thousand Oaks, CA: Sage, 2003.

Padilla, Art, Robert Hogan, and Robert B. Kaiser. "The Toxic Triangle: Destructive Leaders, Susceptible Followers, and Conducive Environments." *Leadership Quarterly* 18, no. 3 (2007): 176–94.

Palmisano, Samuel J. "The Globally Integrated Enterprise." *Foreign Affairs* 85, no. 3 (2006): 127–36.

Peters, Thomas J. "Leadership: Sad Facts and Silver." In *Harvard Business Review on Breakthrough Leadership*, by Daniel Goleman, William Peace, William Pagonis, Tom Peters, Gareth Jones, and Harris Collingwood, 127–50. Boston: Harvard Business School Press, 2001.

Pfeffer, Jeffrey. "The Ambiguity of Leadership." *The Academy of Management Review* 2, no. 1 (1977): 104–12.

Pittinsky, Todd L. "Allophilia and Intergroup Leadership." In *Building Leadership Bridges 2005: Emergent Models of Global Leadership*, edited by Nancy S. Huber and Mark C. Walker, 34–49. College Park, MD: International Leadership Association, 2005.

Pittinsky, Todd L., Laura M. Bacon, and Brian Welle. "The Great Women Theory of Leadership? Perils of Positive Stereotypes and Precarious Pedestals." In *Women and Leadership*, edited by Barbara

Kellerman and Deborah L. Rhode, 93–125. San Francisco: Jossey-Bass, 2007.

Pittinsky, Todd L., R. Matthew Montoya, and Linda R. Tropp. "Leader Influences on Positive and Negative Intergroup Emotions." Paper presented at the Tenth Annual Meeting of Research on Managing Groups and Teams, Cornell and Stanford Universities, May 2006.

Pittinsky, Todd L., and Margaret J. Shih. "Leading the Knowledge Nomad." In *Workforce Wake-Up Call: Your Workforce Is Changing, Are You?* edited by Robert Gandossy, Nidhi Verma, and Elissa Tucker, 95–100. Hoboken, NJ: John Wiley & Sons, 2006.

Podolny, Joel, Rakesh Khurana, and Marya Hill-Popper. "Revisiting the Meaning of Leadership." Unpublished paper, 2004.

Price, Terry L. "Explaining Ethical Failures of Leadership." In *Ethics: The Heart of Leadership*, edited by Joanne B. Ciulla, 129–45. 2nd ed. Westport, CT: Praeger, 2004.

Purkis, Jonathan. "Leaderless Cultures: The Problem of Authority in a Radical Environmental Group." In *Leadership and Social Movements*, edited by Colin Barker, Alan Johnson and Michael Lavalette, 160–77. Manchester: Manchester University Press, 2001.

Reger, Jo. "Introduction: New Dimensions in the Study of Social Movement Leadership." *American Behavioral Scientist* 50, no. 10 (2007): 1303–5.

Roberto, Michael A., and Gina M. Carioggia. "Launching the War on Terrorism." Case No. 9–303–027. Cambridge, MA: Harvard Business School, 2002.

Rosener, Judy B. "Ways Women Lead." *Harvard Business Review* 68, no. 6 (1990): 119–25.

Rosenthal, Seth A., and Todd L. Pittinsky. "Narcissistic Leadership." *The Leadership Quarterly* 17, no. 6 (2006): 617–33.

Salovey, Peter, and John D. Mayer. "Emotional Intelligence." *Imagination, Cognition, and Personality* 9 (1990): 185–211.

Sapolsky, Robert M. "The Influence of Social Hierarchy on Primate Health." *Science* 308, no. 5722 (2005): 648–52.

———. "A Natural History of Peace." *Foreign Affairs* 85, no. 1 (2006): 104–20.

Schein, Edgar H. "Defining Organizational Culture." In *The Leader's Companion: Insight on Leadership through the Ages*, edited by J. Thomas Wren, 271–81. New York: Free Press, 1995.

Schussman, Alan, and Jennifer Earl. "From Barricades to Firewalls? Strategic Voting and Social Movement Leadership in the Internet Age." *Sociological Inquiry* 74, no. 4 (2004): 439–63.

Shamir, Boas. "The Charismatic Relationship: Alternative Explanations and Predictions." *Leadership Quarterly* 2, no. 2 (1991): 81–104.

Shils, Edward. "Charisma, Order, Status." *American Sociological Review* 30 (1965): 199–213.

Simonton, Dean K. "Dispositional Attributions of (Presidential) Leadership: An Experimental Simulation of Historiometric Results." *Journal of Experimental Social Psychology* 22 (1986): 389–418.

———. "Presidential Greatness: The Historical Consensus and Its Psychological Significance." *Political Psychology* 7 (1986): 259–83.

———. "Presidential Personality: Biographical Use of the Gough Adjective Check List." *Journal of Personality and Social Psychology* 51, no. 1 (1986): 149–60.

Snook, Scott, and Rakesh Khurana. "Developing 'Leaders of Character': Lessons from West Point." Unpublished manuscript.

Spencer, Herbert. "The Great Man Theory Breaks Down." In *Political Leadership: A Source Book*, edited by Barbara Kellerman, 10–15. Pittsburgh, PA: University of Pittsburgh Press, 1986.

Stauffer, David. "Boosting Your Emotional Intelligence." *Harvard Management Update* 2, no. 10 (1997): 3–4.

Sternberg, Robert J. "Successful Intelligence: A New Approach to Leadership." In *Multiple Intelligences and Leadership*, edited by Ronald E. Riggio, Susan E. Murphy, and Francis J. Pirozzolo, 9–28. Mahwah, NJ: Lawrence Erlbaum, 2002.

Stogdill, R. M. "Personal Factors Associated with Leadership: A Survey of the Literature." *Journal of Psychology* 25 (1948): 35–71.

Szabo, Erna, Gerhard Reber, Jurgen Weibler, Felix C. Brodbeck, and Rolf Wunderer. "Values and Behavior Orientation in Leadership Studies: Reflections Based on Findings in Three German-Speaking Countries." *Leadership Quarterly* 12 (2001): 219–44.

Tedlow, Richard S. "What Titans Can Teach Us." *Harvard Business Review* 79, no. 11 (2001): 70–79.

Thomas, Alan Berkeley. "Does Leadership Make a Difference to Organizational Performance?" *Administrative Science Quarterly* 33, no. 3 (1988): 388–400.

Thorndike, Edward L. "Intelligence and Its Uses." *Harpers Magazine* 140 (1920): 227–35.

Tourigny, Louise, William L. Dougan, John Washbush, and Christine Clements. "Explaining Executive Integrity: Governance, Charisma, Personality and Agency." *Management Decisions* 41, no. 10 (2003): 1035–49.

Vroom, Victor H. "Leadership and Decision Making Processes." *Organizational Dynamics* 28, no. 4 (2000): 82–94.

Walzer, Michael. "Political Action: The Problem of Dirty Hands." *Philosophy and Public Affairs* 2, no. 2 (1973): 160–80.

Wasserman, Noam, Bharat Anand, and Nitin Nohria. "When Does Leadership Matter? The Contingent Opportunities View of CEO Leadership." Working Paper 01–063. Cambridge, MA: Harvard Business School, April 2001.

Weber, Max. "Politics as a Vocation." In *From Max Weber: Essays in Sociology*, edited by H. H. Gerth and C. Wright Mills, 77–128. New York: Oxford University Press, 1958.

———. "Types of Authority." In *Political Leadership: A Source Book*, edited by Barbara Kellerman, 232–44. Pittsburgh, PA: University of Pittsburgh Press, 1986.

Willis, Janine, and Alexander Todorov. "First Impressions: Making Up Your Mind after a 100-Ms Exposure to a Face." *Psychological Science* 17, no. 7 (2006): 592–98.

Winston, Kenneth. "Necessity and Choice in Political Ethics: Varieties of Dirty Hands." In *Professional Ethics and Social Responsibility*, edited by Daniel E. Wueste, 37–66. Lanham, MD: Rowman & Littlefield, 1994.

Winter, David G. "Leader Appeal, Leader Performance, and the Motive Profiles of Leaders and Followers: A Study of American Presidents and Elections." *Journal of Personality and Social Psychology* 52, no. 1 (1989): 196–202.

Yukl, Gary A. "An Evaluation of Conceptual Weaknesses in Transformational and Charismatic Leadership Theories." *Leadership
Quarterly* 10, no. 2 (1999): 285–305.

Yukl, Gary A., and Cecilia M. Falbe. "The Importance of Different
Power Sources in Downward and Lateral Relations." *Journal of
Applied Psychology* 76 (1991): 416–23.

Yukl, Gary A., and David D. Van Fleet. "Theory and Research on
Leadership in Organizations." In *Handbook of Industrial and Organi-
zational Psychology, Volume 3*, edited by Marvin D. Dunnette and
Leaetta M. Hough, 147–97. 2nd ed. Palo Alto, CA: Consulting
Psychologists Press, 1992.

Zaccaro, Stephen J. "Trait-Based Perspectives of Leadership." *American
Psychologist*, 62, no. 1 (2007): 6–16.

Zaleznik, Abraham. "Managers and Leaders: Are They Different?"
Harvard Business Review 55, no. 3 (1977): 67–78.

Zimbardo, Philip G. "The Psychology of Power: To the Person? To the
Situation? To the System?" In *Moral Leadership: The Theory and
Practice of Power, Judgment and Policy*, edited by Deborah L. Rhode,
129–57. San Francisco: Jossey-Bass, 2006.

Zogby International. "Roosevelt Continues to Dominate Presidential
Greatness Scale." Available as a download from http://www.zogby
.com/news/ReadNews.dbm?ID=1234 (as of August 31, 2007).

Books

Abshire, David M. *Saving the Reagan Presidency: Trust Is the Coin of the
Realm*. College Station: Texas A&M University Press, 2005.

Allen, Mark. *Arabs*. London: Continuum, 2006.

Allison, Graham, and Philip Zelikow. *Essence of Decision: Explaining the
Cuban Missile Crisis*. 2nd ed. New York: Longman, 1999.

Alterman, Eric. *When Presidents Lie: A History of Official Deception and Its
Consequences*. New York: Viking, 2004.

Anderson, Benedict. *Imagined Communities: Reflections on the Origin and
Spread of Nationalism*. Rev. ed. New York: Verso, 1991.

Appiah, Kwame Anthony. *The Ethics of Identity*. Princeton, NJ: Princeton University Press, 2005.

Axelrod, Alan. *Eisenhower on Leadership: Ike's Enduring Lessons in Total Victory Management*. San Francisco: Jossey-Bass, 2006.

Axelrod, Robert M. *The Evolution of Cooperation*. New York: Basic Books, 1984.

Badaracco Jr., Joseph L. *Defining Moments: When Managers Must Choose between Right and Right*. Boston: Harvard Business School Press, 1997.

Barker, Colin, Alan Johnson, and Michael Lavalette, eds. *Leadership and Social Movements*. Manchester: Manchester University Press, 2001.

Barnard, Chester I. *The Functions of the Executive*. Cambridge, MA: Harvard University Press, 1979.

Bass, Bernard M. *Transformational Leadership: Industrial, Military, and Educational Impact*. Mahwah, NJ: Lawrence Erlbaum, 1998.

Blight, James G., and Janet M. Lang. *The Fog of War: Lessons from the Life of Robert S. McNamara*. Lanham, MD: Rowman & Littlefield, 2005.

Boehm, Christopher. *Hierarchy in the Forest: The Evolution of Egalitarian Behavior*. Cambridge, MA: Harvard University Press, 1999.

Brinkley, Douglas. *Rosa Parks*. New York: Penguin Viking Lipper, 2000.

Brown, Judith M. *Nehru: A Political Life*. New Haven, CT: Yale University Press, 2003.

Burns, James MacGregor. *Leadership*. New York: Harper & Row, 1978.
———. *Transforming Leadership: A New Pursuit of Happiness*. New York: Atlantic Monthly Press, 2003.

Burns, James MacGregor, and Susan Dunn. *The Three Roosevelts: Patrician Leaders Who Transformed America*. New York: Grove Press, 2002.

Burt, Ronald S. *Structural Holes: The Social Structure of Competition*. Cambridge, MA: Harvard University Press, 1992.

Cairncross, Frances. *The Death of Distance: How the Communications Revolution Will Change Our Lives*. Boston: Harvard Business School Press, 2001.

Carlyle, Thomas. *On Heroes, Hero Worship, and the Heroic in History*. New York: Ginn, 1902.

Caro, Robert A. *Master of the Senate: The Years of Lyndon Johnson*. New York: Knopf, 2002.

Clippinger, John H. *A Crowd of One: The Future of Individual Identity*. New York: Public Affairs, 2007.

Cohen, Michael D., and James G. March. *Leadership and Ambiguity: The American College President*. Boston: Harvard Business School Press, 1986.

Collins, Jim. *Good to Great: Why Some Companies Make the Leap . . . and Others Don't*. New York: Harper Business, 2001.

Conger, Jay A., and Rabindra N. Kanungo. *Charismatic Leadership in Organizations*. Thousand Oaks, CA: Sage, 1998.

Dahl, Robert A. *Who Governs? Democracy and Power in an American City*. New Haven, CT: Yale University Press, 1961.

Deutsch, Karl W. *The Nerves of Government: Models of Political Communication and Control*. New York: Free Press, 1966.

Doig, Jameson W., and Erwin C. Hargrove, eds. *Leadership and Innovation: Entrepreneurs in Government*. Baltimore, MD: Johns Hopkins University Press, 1990.

Earley, P. Christopher, and Soon Ang. *Cultural Intelligence: Individual Interactions across Cultures*. Stanford, CA: Stanford University Press, 2003.

Edwards, David V. and R. Harrison Wagner, eds. *Political Power: A Reader in Theory and Research*. New York: Free Press, 1969.

Edwards, George. *On Deaf Ears: The Limits of the Bully Pulpit*. New Haven, CT: Yale University Press, 2003.

Friedman, Thomas L. *The World Is Flat: A Brief History of the Twenty-First Century*. New York: Farrar, Straus and Giroux, 2006.

Fung, Archon, and Erik Olin Wright, eds. *Deepening Democracy: Institutional Innovations in Empowered Participatory Governance*. London: Verso, 2003.

Gelernter, David. *Americanism: The Fourth Great Western Religion*. New York: Doubleday, 2007.

George, Bill, with Peter Sims. *True North: Discover Your Authentic Leadership*. San Francisco: Wiley, 2007.

Gergen, David R. *Eyewitness to Power: The Essence of Leadership: Nixon to Clinton*. New York: Simon & Schuster, 2000.

Gibbon, Peter H. *A Call to Heroism: Renewing America's Vision to Greatness*. New York: Atlantic Monthly Press, 2002.

Gladwell, Malcolm. *Blink: The Power of Thinking Without Thinking.* New York: Little, Brown, 2005.

Goffman, Erving. *The Presentation of Self in Everyday Life.* Garden City, NY: Doubleday, 1959.

Goleman, Daniel, Richard E. Boyatzis, and Annie McKee. *Primal Leadership: Learning to Lead with Emotional Intelligence.* Boston: Harvard Business School Press, 2002.

Goodwin, Doris Kearns. *Team of Rivals: The Political Genius of Abraham Lincoln.* New York: Simon & Schuster, 2005.

Greenstein, Fred I. *The Hidden-Hand Presidency: Eisenhower as Leader.* New York: Basic Books, 1982.

———, ed. *The George W. Bush Presidency: An Early Assessment.* Baltimore, MD: Johns Hopkins University Press, 2003.

———. *The Presidential Difference: Leadership Style from FDR to George W. Bush.* 2nd ed. Princeton, NJ: Princeton University Press, 2004.

Grint, Keith. *Leadership: Classical, Contemporary, and Critical Approaches.* Oxford: Oxford University Press, 1997.

———. *The Arts of Leadership.* Oxford: Oxford University Press, 2000.

Haass, Richard N., *The Bureaucratic Entrepreneur: How to Be Effective in Any Unruly Organization.* Washington, DC: Brookings Institution Press, 1999.

Hackman, J. Richard. *Leading Teams. Setting the Stage for Great Performance.* Boston: Harvard Business School Press, 2002.

Harman, Sidney. *Mind Your Own Business.* New York: Currency/ Doubleday, 2003.

Heenan, David A., and Warren G. Bennis. *Co-Leaders: The Power of Great Partnerships.* New York: John Wiley, 1999.

Heifetz, Ronald. *Leadership without Easy Answers.* Cambridge, MA: Belknap Press of Harvard University Press, 1994.

Hesselbein, Frances, and General Eric K. Shinseki. *Be-Know-Do: Leadership the Army Way: Adapted from the Official Army Leadership Manual.* San Francisco: Jossey-Bass, 2004.

Hesselbein, Frances, General Eric K. Shinseki, and Marshall Goldsmith, eds. *The Leader of the Future 2: Visions, Strategies, and Practices for the New Era.* San Francisco: Jossey-Bass, 2006.

Hirschman, Albert O. *Exit, Voice, and Loyalty: Responses to Decline in Firms, Organizations, and States*. Cambridge, MA: Harvard University Press, 1970.

Hodgkinson, Christopher. *The Philosophy of Leadership*. New York: St. Martin's, 1983.

House, Robert J., Paul J. Hanges, Mansour Javidan, Peter W. Dorfman, and Vipin Gupta, eds. *Culture, Leadership, and Organizations: The GLOBE Study of 62 Societies*. Thousand Oaks, CA: Sage, 2007.

Isaacson, Walter. *Einstein: His Life and Universe*. New York: Simon & Schuster, 2007.

Kamarck, Elaine C. *End of Government . . . as We Know It: Making Public Policy Work*. Boulder, CO: Lynne Rienner, 2007.

Kaplan, Robert D. *Warrior Politics: Why Leadership Demands a Pagan Ethos*. New York: Random House, 2002.

Kellerman, Barbara. *Bad Leadership: What It Is, How It Happens, Why It Matters*. Boston: Harvard Business School Press, 2004.

————. *Followership: How Followers Create Change and Change Leaders*. Boston: Harvard Business School Press, 2008.

Kelley, Robert E. *The Power of Followership: How to Create Leaders People Want to Follow, and Followers Who Lead Themselves*. New York: Doubleday/Currency, 1992.

Keohane, Robert O., and Joseph S. Nye. *Power and Interdependence*. Boston: Little Brown, 1977.

Kets de Vries, Manfred F. R. *The Leadership Mystique: An Owner's Manual*. London: Financial Times Prentice-Hall, 2001.

Khurana, Rakesh. *Searching for a Corporate Savior: The Irrational Quest for Charismatic CEOs*. Princeton, NJ: Princeton University Press, 2002.

Kingdon, John W. *Agendas, Alternatives, and Public Policies*. 2nd ed. New York: Longman, 2003.

Kissinger, Henry. *Diplomacy*. New York: Simon & Schuster, 1994.

Klein, Gary. *Sources of Power*. Cambridge, MA: MIT Press, 1999.

Kotter, John P. *Leading Change*. Boston: Harvard Business School Press, 1996.

Krakauer, Jon. *Into Thin Air: A Personal Account of the Mt. Everest Disaster*. New York: Villard, 1998.

Lao Tzu. *Tao Te Ching: A New English Version.* Foreword and notes by Stephen Mitchell. London: Macmillan, 1988.

Lindholm, Charles. *Charisma.* Cambridge, MA: Blackwell, 1990.

Lord, Robert G., and Karen J. Maher. *Leadership and Information Processing: Linking Perceptions and Performance.* Boston: Unwin Hyman, 1991.

Ludwig, Arnold M. *King of the Mountain: The Nature of Political Leadership.* Lexington: University Press of Kentucky, 2002.

Lukes, Steven. *Power: A Radical View.* 2nd ed. London: Palgrave, 2005.

Machiavelli, Niccolò. *The Prince.* New York: New American Library, 1952.

Mansbridge, Jane J. *Beyond Self-Interest.* Chicago: University of Chicago Press, 1990.

Marx, Karl. *The Eighteenth Brumaire of Louis Bonaparte.* New York: International Publishers, 1963.

Mayo, Anthony J., and Nitin Nohria. *In Their Time: The Greatest Business Leaders of the Twentieth Century.* Boston: Harvard Business School Press, 2005.

Moore, Mark H. *Creating Public Value: Strategic Management in Government.* Cambridge, MA: Harvard University Press, 1995.

National Commission on Terrorist Attacks upon the U.S. *9/11 Commission Report, Final Report,* CIS-NO: 2004-J892–23, July 22, 2004, available as a download from http://www.9–11commission.gov/ (as of August 31, 2007).

Neustadt, Richard E. *Presidential Power and the Modern Presidents: The Politics of Leadership from Roosevelt to Reagan.* New York: Free Press, 1990.

Nye Jr., Joseph S. *Bound to Lead: The Changing Nature of American Power.* New York: Basic Books, 1990.

———. *The Power Game: A Washington Novel.* New York: Public Affairs, 2004.

Nye Jr., Joseph S., Philip D. Zelikow, and David C. King, eds. *Why People Don't Trust Government.* Cambridge, MA: Harvard University Press, 1997.

Osborne, David, and Ted Gaebler. *Reinventing Government: How the Entrepreneurial Spirit Is Transforming the Public Sector.* Reading, MA: Addison-Wesley, 1992.

Parks, Sharon Daloz. *Leadership Can Be Taught: A Bold Approach for a Complex World*. Boston: Harvard Business School Press, 2005.

Patten, Chris. *Cousins and Strangers: America, Britain, and Europe in a New Century*. 1st American ed. New York: Times Books, 2006.

Pfeffer, Jeffrey, and Gerald Salancik. *The External Control of Organizations. A Resource Dependence Perspective*. New York: Harper & Row, 1978.

Post, Jerrold M. *Leaders and Their Followers in a Dangerous World: The Psychology of Political Behavior*. Ithaca, NY: Cornell University Press, 2004.

Powell, Gary N. *Women and Men in Management*. 3rd ed. Thousand Oaks, CA: Sage, 2003.

Power, Samantha. *"A Problem from Hell": America and the Age of Genocide*. New York: Basic Books, 2002.

Rawls, John. *Law of Peoples*. Cambridge, MA: Harvard University Press, 1999.

Rhode, Deborah L., ed. *The Difference "Difference" Makes: Women and Leadership*. Stanford, CA: Stanford University Press, 2003.

Roberto, Michael A. *Why Good Leaders Don't Take Yes for an Answer: Managing for Conflict and Consensus*. Upper Saddle River, NJ: Wharton School Publishing, 2005.

Rost, Joseph C. *Leadership for the Twenty-First Century*. Westport, CT: Praeger, 1991.

Salacuse, Jeswald W. *Leading Leaders: How to Manage Smart, Talented, Rich, and Powerful People*. New York: AMACOM, 2006.

Scott, James C. *Domination and the Arts of Resistance: Hidden Transcripts*. New Haven, CT: Yale University Press, 1990.

Shrum, Shirley C., and Linda M. Fedigan, eds. *Primate Encounters: Models of Science, Gender and Society*. Chicago: University of Chicago Press, 2000.

Smith, Adam. *The Theory of Moral Sentiments*. New York: A. M. Kelley, 1966.

Sun Bin. *Sun Bin: The Art of Warfare: A Translation of the Classic Chinese Work of Philosophy and Strategy*. Translated, with an introduction and commentary, by D. C. Lau and Roger T. Ames. Albany: State University of New York Press, 2003.

Taubman, William. *Khrushchev: The Man and His Era*. New York: Norton, 2003.

Taylor, Alan J. P. *Bismarck: The Man and the Statesman.* London: Sutton Publishing, 1955.

Thompson, Charles T. *The Peace Conference Day by Day: A Presidential Pilgrimage Leading to the Discovery of Europe.* New York: Brentano's, 1920.

Traub, James. *The Best Intentions: Kofi Annan and the UN in the Era of American World Power.* New York: Farrar, Straus and Giroux, 2006.

Triandis, Harry C. *Culture and Social Behavior.* New York: McGraw-Hill, 1994.

Tucker, Robert C. *Politics as Leadership.* Rev. ed. Columbia: University of Missouri Press, 1995.

Twain, Mark. *The Adventures of Huckleberry Finn.* New York: Grosset & Dunlap, 1948.

Useem, Michael. *The Leadership Moment: Nine True Stories of Triumph and Disaster and Their Lessons for Us All.* New York: Three Rivers Press, 1998.

Weisband, Edward, and Thomas M. Franck. *Resignation in Protest: Political and Ethical Choices between Loyalty to Team and Loyalty to Conscience in American Public Life.* New York: Penguin, 1975.

Williams, Bernard. *Moral Luck.* Cambridge, MA: Cambridge University Press, 1981.

Williams, Dean. *Real Leadership: Helping People and Organizations Face Their Toughest Challenges.* San Francisco: Berrett-Koehler, 2005.

Willner, Ann Ruth. *The Spellbinders: Charismatic Political Leadership.* New Haven, CT: Yale University Press, 1984.

Wills, Garry. *Certain Trumpets: The Call of Leaders.* New York: Simon & Schuster, 1994.

Woodward, Bob. *State of Denial.* New York: Simon & Schuster, 2006.

Wrangham, Richard, and Dale Peterson. *Demonic Males: Apes and the Origins of Human Violence.* New York: Houghton Mifflin, 1996.

Xenephon. *The Education of Cyrus.* Translated by Henry Graham Dakyns. New York: E. P. Dutton, 1914.

Newspaper and Magazine Articles

Abramowitz, Michael. "Truman's Trials Resonate for Bush." *Washington Post,* December 15, 2006, A3.

Associated Press. "Pentagon Softens Instructor's Role." *Washington Times*, October 11, 2006, 4.

Brooks, David. "Heroes and History." *New York Times*, July 17, 2007, A21.

Brush, Silla. "A Vote of No Confidence." *U.S. News & World Report*, October 30, 2006, 56.

Carey, Benedict. "Brain Injury Said to Affect Moral Choices." *New York Times*, March 22, 2007, A19.

Chivers, C. J. "Behold Turkmenistan's Marvels! (Authorized Version)." *New York Times*, July 19, 2007, A4.

Christensen, Karen. "Putting Power into Practice: An Interview with Rosabeth Moss Kanter." *Rotman Magazine*, Spring/Summer 2005, 14–17.

Cloud, David S. "Here's Donny! In His Defense, a Show Is Born." *New York Times*, April 19, 2006, A1, A15.

Conrad, Annett, Michael Frohlingsdorf, Konstantin von Hammerstein, Horand Knaup, Felix Kurz, Roland Nelles, Christian Reiermann, Michael Sauga, and Gabor Steingart. "Kanzler im Grauschleier" ["Chancellor in Grey Veil"], *Der Spiegel*, October 28, 2002, 20–26.

"Follow My Leader: Why Leadership Makes Britons Queasy." *Economist*, October 23, 2004, 57.

Gapper, John. "Companies Feel Benefit of Intangibles." *Financial Times Special Report on Global Brands*, April 23, 2007, 1.

George, Bill. "Truly Authentic Leadership." *U.S. News & World Report*, October 30, 2006, 52–54.

"Governing Harvard: A *Harvard Magazine* Roundtable." *Harvard Magazine*, May–June 2006, 25–35, and 98–99.

Hernandez, Raymond. "On Podium, Some Say, Mrs. Clinton Is No Mr. Clinton." *New York Times*, February 13, 2006, B3.

Holland, Kelley. "Life after a Merger: Learning on Both Sides." *New York Times*, June 24, 2007, BU21.

Ignatieff, Michael. "Getting Iraq Wrong: What the War Has Taught Me about Political Judgment." *New York Times Magazine*, August 5, 2007, 26–29.

Khurana, Rakesh. "Good Charisma, Bad Business." *New York Times*, September 13, 2002, A27.

Kristol, William. "Why Bush Will Be a Winner." *Washington Post*, July 15, 2007, B1.

Krogh, Egil. "The Break-In That History Forgot." *New York Times*, June 30, 2007, A17.

Krulak, Charles C., and Joseph P. Hoar. "It's Our Cage, Too." *Washington Post*, May 17, 2007, A17.

Lambert, Craig. "Le Professeur." *Harvard Magazine*, July–August, 2007, 32–37.

Landler, Mark. "Chairman to Quit Siemens, Casualty in Graft Accusations." *New York Times*, April 20, 2007, C3.

"The Man behind the Fist." *Economist*, March 31, 2007, 27–30.

Mazzetti, Mark. "Spy Agencies Say Iraq War Worsens Terrorism Threat." *New York Times*, September 24, 2006, 1.

Mintzberg, Henry. "Community-Ship Is the Answer." *Financial Times*, October 23, 2006, 8.

Mulgan, Geoff. "We Need Government—and We Need It to Be Boring." *The Spectator*, May 13, 2006, 17.

Mulrine, Anna. "Emphasizing Ethics Even as Bullets Fly." *U.S. News & World Report*, June 19, 2006, 25–26.

"A Nation Challenged; Scenes of Rejoicing and Words of Strategy from Bin Laden and His Allies." *New York Times*, December 14, 2001, B4.

Nocera, Joe. "Running GE, Comfortable in His Skin." *New York Times*, June 9, 2007, C1, C9.

Noonan, Peggy. "What Nobodies Know." *Wall Street Journal*, March 23, 2006. http://www.opinionjournal.com/columnists/pnoonan/?id=110008126.

"Philosophy and Neuroscience: Posing the Right Question." *Economist*, March 24, 2007, 91–92.

"The Politics of Beauty: Fit to Serve." *Economist*, January 20, 2007, 71.

Portillo, Michael. "Yes, We Will Miss Him; Exit Blair." *International Herald Tribune*, June 23–24, 2007, 8.

Quelch, John. "How Soft Power Is Winning Hearts, Minds, and Influence." *Financial Times*, October 10, 2005, p.17.

Ramesh, Jairam. "Political Legacies." *Economist*, June 23, 2007, 21.

Rawnsley, Andrew. "Tony Blair's Premiership Has Big Lessons for Gordon Brown: Whatever Their Cunning Plans, the Most Tested

Times for Leaders Come from the Shock Events They Never Anticipated." *Observer*, June 24, 2007, 31.

Rothstein, Edward. "Churchill, Heroic Relic or Relevant Now?" *New York Times*, March 29, 2003, D7, D9.

Runciman, David. "Squalls That Await the New Prime Minister." *Financial Times*, June 28, 2007, 13.

"Saddam Hussein: The Blundering Dictator." *Economist*, January 6, 2007, 39–40.

Shanker, Thom. "Retiring Army Chief of Staff Warns against Arrogance." *New York Times*, June 12, 2003, A32.

———. "Study Is Said to Find Overlap in U.S. Counterterror Effort." *New York Times*, March 18, 2006, A8.

Skapinker, Michael. "Leadership Shakes off the Liability of Charisma." *Financial Times*, October 10, 2001, p.15.

"Slobodan Milosevic." *Economist*, March 18, 2006, 83.

Smolin, Lee. "The Other Einstein." *New York Review of Books*, June 14, 2007, 76–83.

Stack, Megan K. "He Was More Symbol Than Sweeping Leader." *Los Angeles Times*, June 9, 2006, 1.

Stephens, Philip. "Hubris Is the Thread Running through Blair's Many Travails." *Financial Times*, July 14, 2006, 15.

———. "Ten Years on, a New Set of Rules." *Financial Times*, May 1, 2007, 13.

Stolberg, Sheryl Gay. "For President Bush, a Reversal of Fortune on His Political Control." *New York Times*, June 30, 2007, A11.

Vara, Vauhini. "Boss Talks (a Special Report)—After GE: Intuit's Steve Bennett on Why Some General Electric Alumni Succeed—and Some Don't." *Wall Street Journal*, April 16, 2007, R3, R7.

Wilkerson, Lawrence B. "The White House Cabal." *Los Angeles Times*, October 25, 2005, B11.

Index

Page numbers followed by *t* indicate tables.

physical appearance, 15–16, 60–61
Piccolo, Ronald F., 165n30
Pied Piper, 18–19, 142
Pierer, Heinrich von, 106
Pirozzolo, Francis J., 166n37, 171nn5, 15
Pittinsky, Todd L., 161n61, 163n81,
  175n2, 180n59
Plato, 10
Platow, Michael J., 176n13, 177n58
Platt, Gerald M., 179n57
pluralism, 127
Podolny, Joel, 179n54
Poindexter, John, 79
police, 29, 41
political capital, 80
political culture, 1, 3, 9–10, 96–100,
  137–39
  alpha male theory of leadership and,
  12
  charisma and, 53, 54–60
  communications skills and, 72
  cultural limits on power and, 36–37,
  96
  instant global communication and,
  47–48
  leadership style and, 68
  leadership traits and, 15, 19, 36, 41
  networks and, 45, 50
  physical appearance and, 61
  soft power and, 36, 37, 42, 43, 63, 82,
  140–45
  sources of power in, 29–30, 36, 43
  transformational leaders and, 7–9, 126
  See also democracies; dictators;
  presidents, U.S.
political intelligence, 80
political skills, 11, 80–84, 83t, 88, 145,
  148
Pol Pot, 130
popularity, 42
Popular Revolutionary Army (EPR),
  92, 93
positional power, 42

Post, Jerrold M., 164n10, 174n48
Powell, Colin, 79, 106, 138
Powell, Enoch, 178n38
Powell, Gary N., 162n75
power, ix–x, xii, 25, 27–52
  bad leadership and, 111
  bullying and, 81–82
  charismatic leaders and, 58
  combination of resources for, 84
  context and, 27, 67, 85
  definitions of, 27, 28
  distribution of resources for, 96–100
  fallacies of, 28
  of followers, 32–37
  limited domains of, 28
  motivations for, 109–10, 143
  networks and, 44–52
  restraint in use of, 81–82
  situational leadership and, 32–33
  three legitimated types of, 37
  tools of, 27–28
  transformational leaders and, 61–62, 66
  See also hard power; soft power
Power, Samantha, 180n64
power strategy, 84
practical knowledge, 148
pragmatic followers, 34, 68t
pragmatic leaders, 67, 67t
preferences, establishment of, 30–31
presidents, U.S.
  charisma and, 59–60
  crisis conditions and, 68
  deception and, 121, 122
  as eventful vs. event-making leaders,
  7–8, 9
  greatness ratings of, 125
  informal/formal powers and, 32, 43
  legitimate power of, 38
  Machiavellianism and, 82
  objectives and style of, 65, 66t
  organizational skills of, 77–80
  public vs. private morality and,
  114–15, 118–19

soft power, x, xii, 1, 2, 29–32, 33, 34, 87,
    147
  business success and, 49
  charisma and, xi, 53–54, 55, 65, 83t,
    143, 147
  conditions for, 68
  context and, 67
  currency of, 31
  definition of, 29
  follower empowerment and, 140
  hard power mixed with, x, 37–44, 40t,
    63–64, 143, 147
  leaders' styles and, 65
  political culture and, 36, 37, 42, 43,
    63, 82, 140–45
  resources of, 65
  skills of, 69–74, 81, 83t, 130, 145
  transformational leaders and, 62, 63,
    64, 130
  uses of, 43, 52, 140
  warrior-style leadership and, 11
Sosik, John J., 164n12
Soviet Union, 7–8, 12, 33, 37
Speer, Albert, 33
Spencer, Herbert, 5, 151n15
Spony, G., 173n33
sports coaches, 3
Stalin, Joseph, 12, 33, 37, 42,
    73, 107
status quo leaders, 66–67, 74, 130
Stauffer, David, 182n85
Staw, Barry M., 164n15
Steingart, Gabor, 168n60
Stephens, Philip, 151n19, 178n39
Sternberg, Robert J., 166n37, 167n65,
    171n15
Stockholm syndrome, 39
strategy
  contextual intelligence and, 88–89
  definition and resources of, 84
street smarts, 89
Stresemann, Gustav, 57
stress, 103

subordinates. *See* followers
Suez Crisis, 63
Sukarno, 57
Summers, Larry, 82, 84
Sunbeam Corporation, 113
Sun-Tzu, 11
surveys, 23
symbols, 73
system design, 78, 105, 148
Szabo, Erna, 173n34

Taliban, 7
tallness, 15
task-orientation, 21, 87
Taubman, William, 152n34
Taylor, Alan P., 171n10
team leaders, 4, 20, 23, 78, 82, 87
  information flows and, 106
  risks and, 123
Tedlow, Richard S., 159n41
terrorists, 2, 11, 12, 31, 41, 116
  charisma and, 55
  Internet use by, 47
  response to hard power by, 42
  See also September 11 attacks
Thatcher, Margaret, 7, 41, 81
Thomas, Alan Berkeley, 151n12
Thompson, Charles T., 175n56
Thompson, Dennis, 178n30
Thorndike, Edward L., 69, 166n42
threats, 27, 29, 31, 39, 62, 142
Thurman, James, 152n31
ties, weak vs. strong, 45
time-urgent crises, 102–3
Todorov, Alexander, 165n21
torture, 116
Tourigny, Louise, 179nn49, 50
Toyota, 48, 49
trade-offs, 118, 122
traditional authority, 37
training
  of leaders, 4, 14, 24–25, 144–45
  by leaders, 29